D0465844

THE
CHILD
WHO
NEVER
GREW

by Pearl S. Buck

Woodbine House 1992

Second edition, 1992

Cover illustration and design: Liz Wolf

Library of Congress Cataloging-in-Publication Data

Buck, Pearl S. (Pearl Sydenstricker), 1892–1973.
    The child who never grew / by Pearl S. Buck ; foreword by James A. Michener. — 2nd ed.
        p. cm.
    ISBN 0–933149–49–2 : $14.95
    1. Buck, Pearl S. (Pearl Sydenstricker), 1892–1973. 2. Parents of handicapped children—United States—Biography. 3. Mentally handicapped children—United States—Family relationships. 4. Mothers and daughters—United States. I. Title.
HQ759.913.B83 1992
363.3'3'092—dc20   92–34844
[B]   CIP

Printed in the United States of America

10 9 8 7 6 5 4 3 2 1

Contents

Foreword
James A. Michener

For some years at the close of World War II, three people who took writing seriously chanced to live near one another in an attractive corner of eastern Pennsylvania. Centering on the handsome rural town of Doylestown and not far from the artists' colony at New Hope, their homes formed an isosceles triangle. At the southwest corner lived Oscar Hammerstein, gifted lyricist of many New York musical shows, and Pulitzer Prize winner in 1949 for the hugely successful *South Pacific*. Due north of him, eleven miles distant, I lived with my own prize in 1948 for having written the book on which the play was based. And eight miles to the west of each of us stood the stately but not ostentatious home of the famous Pearl Buck, winner of the Pulitzer in 1932 and the Nobel in 1938, both for her tremendously appealing novel *The Good Earth*.

We knew one another favorably, and by coincidence each of us had a strong connection with Asia. Pearl Buck's prizewinning novel dealt with the agrarian peasants of China. Oscar Hammerstein's Australian wife had a sister married to a Japanese, and I would soon have a Japanese wife, but she was born in Colorado and so had always had American citizenship, a fact which did not keep her from being interned in a camp during the war against Japan.

As we three met, and Miss Buck and I could be termed 'old Asia hands,' she brought to our attention the sad and sorry plight of babies who had been sired by American men in military uniform serving in Japan and Korea and then abandoned by their fathers and, shockingly often, by their mothers too. When such babies were either born in the United States or found their way here by devious routes, they were treated no better. As Pearl described to Oscar and me when she invited us to her farm one afternoon: "In our country if the children are totally abandoned, they're most often thrown into some institution for the mentally defective, and there they run the risk of becoming truly retarded. They are doomed."

"Why aren't they put up for adoption?" Oscar asked, and she cried: "That's why I invited you over. Because they're half-white, half-Oriental, it's always been assumed that they're ineligible for adoption. No one tries to place them, and in the institutions they're thrown into they wither."

"That's awful," Hammerstein mumbled, for he was a man with a generous heart, and I seconded his castigation of such a system, but I doubt if either of us would have done much to alleviate it had not Miss Buck with that grim, fearless determination which had always marked her—she did not accept defeat easily—made this announcement: "I have not the slightest doubt in the world that these adorable babies are adoptable. And I propose to find them homes."

"Where will you locate Japanese-American couples who might take the babies?" Hammerstein asked, and she surprised us by snapping:"We won't worry about finding such marriages. We'll place these lovable children in ordinary white homes, like yours or mine."

"Will such people adopt half-caste babies?"

"We'll no longer use that terribly pejorative term. Oscar, we're all half-castes, one way or another. Portuguese-German parents, Russian-English, Swedish-Spanish. That is, if you go back far enough."

And from that meeting and others like it, Pearl Buck with her iron will and the royalties from the blizzard of her books sold by her publisher husband, Richard Walsh of the John Day Company, launched Welcome House, a meticulously run orphanage for unadoptable Asian-American children, most of them fathered by American G.I.s.

In this way Hammerstein and I became deeply involved in finding homes for healthy, normal Eurasian babies—that is, father an American G.I., mother an Asian woman of Japanese, Korean, or Thai heritage—but we did not realize that we were unknowingly edging into a much bigger and more involved problem; the care and nurturing of children who through no fault of their own had mental retardation, children who are born physically competent but whose minds mysteriously stop growing. This book and my foreword deal with the heroic efforts Pearl Buck made to salvage these children, but how Hammerstein and I learned she was engaged in this greater problem will be explained shortly. For the moment we are still concentrating on the ordinary child, the abandoned offspring of the war.

When we launched our serious attempt to find the G.I. babies, we accumulated startling numbers, for traditional adoption agencies were glad to be rid of them, still convinced that they would never find homes in the United States. Pearl Buck worked tirelessly to convince ordinary American families—both husband and wife often Anglo-Saxon white—that her children, as she called them, would make fine additions to their families. She was remarkable in her energy, convincing in her persuasiveness. Before we had been in existence even half a year, she was finding one standard American family after another eager to accept these children.

In her campaign she was wonderfully assisted by the children, for they were adorable, laughing girls and sturdy boys. Sometimes their skin coloring and eye formation favored their Oriental mothers so that they were clearly Eurasian, but just as often it was their fathers' genes that prevailed, and then it was difficult to guess their ancestry. But the important point is that during the years that Hammerstein and I helped her, we found ourselves with not one baby that was unadoptable. True, the fame of Miss Buck as a crusading writer sped the process of finding homes, but in our own less spectacular ways Hammerstein and I helped.

I must stress that much of the hard work, and the monetary contributions to Welcome House, came not from Hammerstein and me. Miss Buck had organized a powerful committee of her neighbors throughout the area to help, and it was they who kept Welcome House functioning. They were valiant assistants, not one of them with any affiliation to Asia. They made their crucial contributions because they were people of good heart.

However, Hammerstein and I were of critical assistance when our venture ran into a secondary obstacle which seemed insurmountable. When we accepted any abandoned child that the other agencies felt they could not place in a stable home, we found that a surprising percentage of them were the offspring of black military fathers and the Oriental women with whom they had lived while in Japan, Korea or Thailand. "These unfortunate children," said the agencies who passed them along to us, "really are unadoptable," and they wished us well after thanking us for having relieved them of a burden they could not handle.

Pearl Buck's finest hour, so far as I witnessed her in action, came when she said with great force: "We welcome these half-black children. They'll prove just as adoptable as the white-Oriental babies you originally told us were unadoptable. The simple fact is, you haven't tried to place them." And she became a heroic propagandist in convincing white married couples that these handsome, dark-skinned babies would mature into adults of whom the family would be proud. Through her unceasing pressure and brimming confidence, she found homes for every black-Oriental orphan who came our way, one of the triumphs of this remarkable woman.

Hammerstein had been deeply involved in these experiences when time came for him to write lyrics for the songs in *South Pacific*, and it could well have been his observation of Pearl Buck at work which inspired him to write one of the famous songs in the play. Joe Cable, the Marine lieutenant from Philadelphia's Main Line and Princeton, is explaining why he cannot marry Liat, his Tonkinese sweetheart. In bitterly specific words, he sings that racial prejudice is not inherited, it is taught. Prior to the play's opening on Broadway, several well-intentioned people approached me, begging that I advise Rodgers and Hammerstein to drop that song, because in a musical show which was supposed to be entertaining, it would grate. Adamantly Hammerstein refused: "That's what the play is about," and when Rodgers supported him, that song became one of the favorable talking points in the play.

At about this time I was allowed an oblique glimpse of Pearl Buck, that is, a view of her contribution that came by accident from an unprejudiced source. While on a writing assignment in Tokyo I received a cable from Miss Buck asking me to visit a Mrs. Renzo Sawada, who had organized her own orphanage to care for abandoned Japanese babies. A woman from a distinguished family, she was highly regarded throughout Japan as a person of compassion and charitable instinct. She had accomplished wonders in finding homes in Japan for her children, but since the Japanese are among the most xenophobic of all national groups—they tend to distrust and fear anyone not pure Japanese—she had found it extremely difficult to place the fair-skinned children of white American G.I.s and totally impossible to locate homes for the offspring of our black G.I.s.

"That's why Mrs. Buck is so valuable to us," Mrs. Sawada told me when I visited her in the spacious family home that contained her orphanage. "Through her courage in the United States we're able to find homes for children who would never find a place if they remained in Japan. Forbidden."

"How do you get the children to us?"

"That's part of the miracle. Mrs. Buck raises funds in the States, sends the money to us, and we fly our babies to you. When I was in the States I saw them arriving at Seattle. Most of them had already been assured a place in one of your families. By using photographs."

"Mrs. Buck directed me to tell you 'Send us all you have. We'll find homes for them,'" and when I left, Mrs. Sawada said: "Without her help, our G.I. babies would be lost. Here there's no place for them."

As I worked with Miss Buck on her gallant venture I gradually became aware that she had a child of her own whom I never saw, a daughter I was told, and it was whispered that this girl was so retarded that she had been spirited away in some refuge for such children. Since I had learned from my work with Pearl that she was acutely reticent about talking of herself, I never asked her about a daughter who might have been impaired; and she certainly never mentioned the matter to me. Nor, because of my travels overseas, was I aware that she had written a magazine article about this family misfortune. No one mentioned it to me, because in our community this was a guarded topic, but when I heard the rumors I did recall what Pearl had told me at our first meeting: "The unwanted children are most often thrown into some institution intended for the mentally defective, and there they run the risk of becoming truly retarded," and from that bitter assessment I deduced that she knew something about the hideously named "insane asylums" in which the G.I. babies were so often hidden away, thus surrendering any hope of normal development.

In late 1951 a neighbor gave me a copy of *The Child Who Never Grew*, the hard-cover book based on the magazine article, and in it I read the harrowing account of how, step by agonizing step, a watchful mother awakens to the fact that her child's mental growth has arbitrarily stopped at a given point, as if a steel curtain has descended about the brain, cutting it off forever from the sentient world about it. Any intellectual communication has became impossible, although the body in which the damaged brain exists survives and even prospers.

When I inquired locally about the book I was told: "Its effect has been phenomenal. Highest praise. Many printings. Because it opened to public discussion a problem that had been previously kept as a shameful secret in the closet of more families than you could ever have anticipated. It was one of the most influential books she wrote." It is for this new edition of her spiritually moving book that I write this introduction.

Thanks to the original edition, I now understood the secret of Pearl Buck's drive to save damaged children. Most were less crippled mentally than her daughter, but each was disadvantaged in her or his own way. Watching her work at saving children, I felt increasing admiration for this gallant woman. However, she and I did not speak of her hidden daughter, until one morning, years later, when Welcome House was a thriving orphanage, still placing every abandoned child that came our way. Early one morning she telephoned me from her home: "James, can you spend the day with me, please? We need to talk." And she proposed that her chauffeur meet me at a rural crossroads.

Unable to guess why she was using this device for an ordinary meeting, I agreed, and when the long black car pulled up I saw that in the back seat rode Pearl Buck, then in her early seventies I believe, regal as always, smiling in friendship and eager to talk. As I settled down for what would be a long drive she said: "On this day I wanted companionship. These days whenever I go to South Jersey I wonder if it will be the last time I shall see her," and she mentioned the quiet little town in southern New Jersey where the refuge stood in which her daughter Carol, now in her forties, had lived for many decades. "It's the best institution of its kind in America. Wonderfully caring people who bring the ultimate out of every child who lives with them."

When I made no comment she continued: "Recent studies by nutrition experts seem to indicate that some chemical deficiency in the first few weeks of life, or perhaps even in the womb during the last month of pregnancy, limited my daughter's ability to nurture her brain cells. And this dooms any child with such a deficiency to a stunted intellectual growth." Having said this, she looked straight ahead for some minutes, then punched her right fist into her left palm and said: "How terrible, to think that the absence of some pill no longer than this might condemn a child to perpetual infancy!" She shook her head in disbelief that such a monstrous event could happen, almost by chance.

And for the rest of the trip south she talked about other advances in the genesis and care of children like her daughter.

When we reached the Training School at Vineland I did not see Carol, now a grown woman, for Pearl did not want a stranger like me to confuse her. Pearl spent about two hours with her daughter, leaving me to read in the limousine. Officials of the home, hearing that I was on the grounds, came to extend courtesies but it was clear to me that Mrs. Buck hoped I would stay where I was, and I did.

At the start of the trip back to Buck's County, Pearl was at first silent, as if the perpetual grief that haunted her over the loss of her child was too poignant to express or share, but after we had traveled some miles in silence, her enthusiasm for life and her constant willingness to face the challenges ahead resumed control, and she talked of her plans for Welcome House and its importation across the Pacific of new groups of Korean-American children who had been abandoned in that country.

During the entire day's trip, although she was fifteen years older than I, she was the one who was more alert, more cogent in her observations and more excited about the future. It was a revealing visit with a brilliant woman in complete control of her mental processes and her plans for continued work. I make this point because some observers have spread the rumor that in her later years Pearl Buck had begun to lose her mental acuity, or perhaps her constant drive toward the future. I can testify that when I last saw her this was not the case. She was more in command than I and on a higher level of intensity.

That was the last time I would see her, and I was glad it had been in such a varied setting: the long drive through beautiful countryside, the prolonged conversation about orphaned children, the revelations about her fears regarding a parent's possible culpability for a child's mental retardation, the love she showed for her daughter, and her plans for continued effort in these fields of adoption and mental retardation in which she had done such superlative work.

It was she alone who conceived the possibility of rescuing Japanese-American orphans from institutions for the mentally retarded and placing them in normal homes. It was she, persevering against advice from those with greater experience, who modified adoption practices. And it was she who supported the efforts of doctors, nurses and welfare experts who were striving to treat people with mental retardation more humanely and with greater insight into the causes and course of mental impairment. She wrote many fine books and won notable prizes, but her major humanitarian work was with children, some of them sadly stigmatized like her own daughter.

Texas Center for Writers
Austin, Texas

Introduction
Martha M. Jablow*

The Child Who Never Grew was published first as an article in the *Ladies Home Journal* in May, 1950, and a year later in hardcover by The John Day Company.

Why would anyone care to read a four-decade old book about a mentally retarded child who was born in 1920? Why would a publisher reissue such a book? Even with a Pulitzer and Nobel prize-winning author, a foreword by James Michener, and an attractive new cover, surely a book written more than forty years ago must be outdated.

"Outdated" and "Pearl Buck" do not belong in the same sentence. Pearl Buck was a woman well ahead of her time—on issues of civil rights, feminism, mental retardation, and children's rights. Yet it is true that some parts of *The Child Who Never Grew* are no longer appropriate or accurate. Since 1950, advances in medicine, education, and law have improved opportunities for people with mental retardation. But the end of this short book addresses the pros and cons of public and private custodial institutions. Many of those huge state institutions which have "an immense advantage in that they are permanent, and once a child enters he is secure for life," as Ms. Buck wrote then, are now closed or closing. The children who were placed there decades ago are adults today living in small group

---

*   Martha Moraghan Jablow is the author of *Cara, Growing with a Retarded Child* (Temple University Press, 1982) and three other non-fiction books.

homes scattered throughout their communities. Many of them are holding jobs, voting, and paying taxes.

The few outdated references in this book are far over-shadowed by Pearl Buck's moving portrayal of parents' conflicting emotions as they come to terms with a child's limitations. When she writes from her heart about her personal pain and struggle with her daughter Carol's con-dition, her voice is universal. She speaks to all parents who have traveled the same road—or who are just embarking on that journey as they discover that their child has some form of developmental delay.

Woodbine House's decision to reissue *The Child Who Never Grew* is based on the book's double value: it is not only supportive to parents in a heartfelt way, but it is also a landmark in the literature about disabilities (a field in which Woodbine House has published several dozen books).

When she wrote *The Child Who Never Grew* in 1950, Pearl Buck was the first prominent person to acknowledge publicly a child with mental retardation. Until then, many families "put the child away" in a caretaking institution, told friends and neighbors that the child had died, and tried to forget that the child existed. Other families quietly kept the child at home, indoors for most of the day, with only limited and chaperoned contact with the outside world.

Because its causes were not well understood at the time, mental retardation also carried a shameful stigma—a dis-grace that was usually shrouded in secrecy, shame, and taboo. Part of the stigma was an erroneous belief that the cause was somehow the family's fault. But by the mid-point of the twentieth century, medical science could shed a glimmer of light to correct some of the misunderstanding. As Ms. Buck wrote, ". . . the majority are retarded from non-inherited causes. The old stigma of 'something in the family' is all too often unjust."

For families whose lives were haunted by the sad mystery of mental retardation, all the scientific explanations in the world would not have as much impact as a famous, respected person disclosing publicly, "I speak as one who knows." In the 1990s' tell-all atmosphere of celebrities baring their most private scars, it may be difficult to appreciate how much courage it took for Pearl Buck to speak out in 1950. But it was a painfully courageous act at that time.

Pearl Buck is the only American woman to receive both the Pulitzer and the Nobel prizes. (The Pulitzer in 1932 for *The Good Earth* and the Nobel prize for literature in 1938.) When a woman of such prestige and achievement "went public" about having a mentally retarded child, the floodgates burst open. She received mailbags of letters from readers whose lives, like hers, had been affected by mental retardation. Some readers even showed up on her doorstep to meet her personally, and she patiently took time to talk with them.

Pearl Buck's lifting the curtain about Carol certainly did not erase entirely the stigma of mental retardation, but it was a watershed. And for that reason, it needs to be placed in historical perspective.

Mental retardation has always been with us. In prehistoric times, people believed that a mental disability was caused by evil spirits—to be driven out by magical rites or potions. The ancient Greeks interpreted it as a punishment from the gods. In some cases, prayer and sacrifices were offered as attempted cure. In other instances, mentally retarded persons were killed or abandoned to die. The Romans regarded them as fools. By the Middle Ages, when belief in witchcraft was rampant in Europe, retarded people were thought to be witches and were tortured, burned, killed, or imprisoned. Some were treated as clowns or jesters, useful only for a hearty laugh.

The Age of Reason (1600s and 1700s) began to sow some seeds of enlightenment about how children learn, which would eventually lead to an understanding of how disabled children also can learn. The groundwork was laid by Jean-Jacques Rousseau, who proposed that children's senses could be used as concrete tools to teach skills. In 1800, a young Parisian physician named Jean-Marc-Gaspard Itard studied Victor, "the wild boy of Aveyron." Thought to be about twelve years old when he was discovered naked and living alone in the woods, Victor had no spoken language. He had apparently been left to die in infancy, his throat partly cut. Itard, who was to become known as the father of child psychology, poked, prodded, and challenged Victor in an attempt to jolt him from his savage state into civilization. Using a metal alphabet, Itard taught Victor to spell the French word for milk, as he drank a glass of *lait.* Victor never learned to speak, but he learned both to recognize and spell certain words. If Itard showed him a flashcard with the word *chaussure,* Victor could find a particular shoe. Victor also learned to read and write verbs and adjectives to communicate in brief sentences. Itard's great achievement was showing that a "defective" child could indeed concentrate and learn. He had potential. He was not an idiot. But Itard's work with Victor was clearly an exception in his time. For the most part, European society placed people who were mentally retarded, deaf, insane, or epileptic with criminals in asylums.

Edouard Seguin, a student of Itard, took the investigation of Victor and human communication a bit further. Seguin contended that mental deficiency was a pedagogical rather then a medical problem. He developed a series of exercises to help a retarded child's motor development. And only a few decades after Victor was discovered, kindergartens sprang up in Germany, based on Friedrich Froebel's belief that very young children could blossom like flowers if schools offered educational toys as intellectual stimulation. While Seguin and Froebel's advances did not pertain specifically to children with mental delays, their insights eventually would prove applicable.

By the 1860s, medical science was taking a harder look at people with signs of mental retardation. Dr. J. Langdon Down, an English physician, first systematically described in 1866 the condition known today as Down syndrome (formerly and unfortunately known as mongolism), the most common type of mental retardation.

The twentieth century brought further understanding. Dr. Maria Montessori, Italy's first female physician, began a demonstration program in 1900 with twenty-two children who were believed to be incapable of learning. Adapting Itard and Sequin's sensory teaching materials, Dr. Montessori showed that these "deficients," as they were called, could indeed learn. In fact, they could pass exams on a level with normal children. Based on that experience, Dr. Montessori opened a school for normal children in the slums of Rome in 1907 and subsequently established schools around the world for children of all abilities.

In the first quarter of the twentieth century, Western society also toyed with social Darwinism—the theory that the most fit should not only survive but lead. If groups or nations were to become stronger by promoting the most talented individuals, what place could be left for the weaker members of society, like the mentally retarded? Only recently it has come to light in Britain that Winston Churchill used social Darwinism to suggest that the "mentally degenerate" should be forcibly sterilized. As British Home Secretary in 1910-1911, Churchill proposed that this solution would be more humane than concentrating them in institutions. In other words, prevent the degenerates from reproducing and the British empire could eliminate its feebleminded population. Churchill's idea never took hold in Great Britain, but it ironically foreshadowed actions of his nation's enemy, Adolf Hitler.

Meanwhile, the pioneering discoveries of Itard, Seguin, Froebel, Montessori, and a few physicians like Down would languish for decades before being applied to a broad population of children and adults with mental retardation. In the first half of the twentieth century, most were isolated at home, cared for as best a family could, treated as perpetual children and rarely challenged educationally, vocationally, or socially. Or they were sent to large institutions where they were warehoused, often with patients who were mentally ill or criminally insane. Institutions established early in this century carried pejorative names like "institutions for the feeble-minded."

Into this world climate, Caroline Grace Buck was born on March 4, 1920. She would be known within the family as Carol, but she would be a secret from the world for thirty years. Even then, her mother would refer to Carol in her writing as "the child" or "my child," never by name.

Carol was Pearl and John Lossing Buck's first child, born in China where he taught agricultural science and she taught English under the auspices of an American Missionary board. At seven pounds, eight ounces, Carol was a healthy baby with ". . . lots of dark hair, pretty and very alert . . . so alert, looking around," wrote a family friend at the time. During the first three years of Carol's life, Pearl Buck had no hint of a problem.

In August of 1921, as Pearl Buck was mothering seventeen-month-old Carol in China, Franklin Delano Roosevelt was taking a dip in the frigid Bay of Fundy, on the other side of the globe. He soon fell ill with a chill and fever. Within a few days he could not walk or move his legs. After three years of agonizing effort, FDR's struggle with paralysis culminated at the 1924 Democratic National Convention. In his first public appearance since being stricken by polio, FDR walked erect to the podium. Wearing heavy steel braces and supported on one side by a crutch and on the other by his son's arm, FDR reached the podium to thunderous cheers. After a speech nominating Al Smith, FDR was cheered for an hour and thirteen minutes.

Whether Pearl Buck learned of FDR's triumph at the time, through newspaper accounts or letters from friends in America, is merely speculative. But FDR's example of confronting a handicap directly, and in public, would have an eventual impact on her.

Back in China . . . Carol was physically strong and vigorous and showed remarkable musical ability. But as she played and smiled through her first five or six years, it gradually became apparent that her mental development was slower than other children's. After frustrating consultations with doctors in China, Pearl brought Carol to the United States for evaluation. The American doctors' diagnosis was severe mental retardation.

Whenever parents are told that their child has a developmental disability, they wonder *why* and *what*— Why my child? Why our family? What caused it? What could I have done to prevent it? In *The Child Who Never Grew*, Ms. Buck wrote eloquently of these wrenching questions. But in the 1920s and for two more decades, she could take no consolation from a clear reason for Carol's retardation, for there was no explanation. All a doctor could tell her at the time was "I don't know. Somewhere along the way, before birth or after, growth stopped."

Without any explanation or treatment for Carol, Pearl Buck struggled to accept her daughter's condition. As the child of missionaries, Pearl Buck spent most of life in China, steeped in Chinese language and culture. From the Chinese she absorbed two important attitudes: "love of children for their own sakes and beyond" and acceptance of "any human infirmity for what it is," she later wrote. Growing up in China, Ms. Buck saw blind, lame, deformed people coming and going in their communities. No shame, no blame. They were openly "accepted for themselves" because the Chinese believed that any affliction was part of one's fate, ordained by heaven, to be respected as such, and therefore not the fault of the individual or the family.

While this side of Chinese philosophy helped her somewhat to accept Carol's limitations, Pearl Buck fought another Chinese custom: the practice of abandoning female babies. A year before Carol's birth, she had written home about "how much infanticide goes on this city. It is very prevalent over all China. . . . "

By the late 1920s, China was torn by political turmoil—a dangerous and frightening fact which complicated the Bucks' dilemma about Carol and her future. How would they raise this child whose mind seemed to stop growing? What would happen to her if anything happened to them? Who would care for Carol? After much agonizing and searching, Ms. Buck decided to place Carol at age nine in a residential institution, the Training School at Vineland, New Jersey.

While Carol remained safely at Vineland, the world rolled along. In the 1930s and 1940s, Hitler sent mentally retarded people off to camps and ovens. In the same decades, Pearl Buck became a world renowned author. Her most widely read book, *The Good Earth*, is the story of Wang Lung, a peasant who founded a powerful dynasty.

The vast majority of readers never suspected that Wang Lung's sorrow "that his eldest girl child neither spoke nor did those things which were right for her age. . . ." was drawn from the author's life.

With the huge success of *The Good Earth*, the public wanted to know more about Pearl Buck—just who was this American woman living in China? At her publisher's request, she penned a brief biographical sketch, "but I could not mention Carol," she wrote to her closest friend, Emma Edmunds White. And she asked Ms. White not to discuss Carol publicly: "It is not shame at all but something private and sacred, as sorrow must be. I am sore to the touch there and I cannot endure even the touch of sympathy. Silence is best and far the easiest for me. I suppose this is because I am not resigned and never can be. I endure it because I must, but I am not resigned. So make no mention of her and so spare me."

Carol's existence was clouded not only in obscurity but also in error of gender. In 1935, when Pearl Buck married Richard Walsh, her publisher, after divorcing Lossing Buck, *The New York Times'* report of the marriage referred to her as "the mother of a son, 15, and a daughter, 10, by her first marriage." (The ten-year-old daughter was Janice Buck, now Janice C. Walsh, who wrote the Afterword for this revised edition.)

Pearl Buck also wrote a highly autobiographical novel, *The Time Is Noon*, in the mid-1930s, but it was considered too personal to publish. It would have revealed much about the author's life—including "an inadequate first marriage," as she called it, and the retarded child whose existence she worked so hard to conceal from her public. *The Time Is Noon* was not published until 1967.

As Carol adjusted to life at Vineland and her mother wrote prolifically, other developments were occurring that would affect later generations of mentally retarded children. For example, between 1921 and 1932, the Iowa PreSchool Laboratory studied children who entered pre-school at an average age of forty-two months. The study found that they had a mean gain of sixteen IQ points over an eighteen-month stay in preschool. Later tests demonstrated that their IQ gains could be maintained for an average of twelve years if they stayed in school.

Another study that would provide further evidence of the benefits of early childhood education was published in 1930 by researchers H. M. Skeele and H. B. Dye. For their small but significant study, presented to the American Association on Mental Deficiency, Skeele and Dye selected thirteen orphans under age three with an average IQ of 64. The children were moved from their orphanage to an institution for the mentally retarded where older patients and attendants offered them social and mental stimulation. Another group of twelve children, with an average IQ of 87.6, composed a control group and remained in the non-stimulating environment of the orphanage.

After eighteen months of living in the more stimulating atmosphere with adults, the first group gained 27.5 IQ points. After thirty months of languishing in the orphanage, the second group's average IQ *dropped* an average of 26.2 IQ points.

Skeele and Dye kept track of these children and, twenty-one years later, did a follow-up study. All thirteen in the first group had become self-supporting, all had moved out of institutions for the retarded, and their average level of schooling was twelfth grade. Of the twelve in the second, unstimulated group, five still remained in institutions (though one had died), and the group's average school level was third grade.

It would be another generation before Skeele and Dye's research findings would be applied to wider practice. By demonstrating that early stimulation can accelerate a child's cognitive growth and a lack of stimulation hinders it, their work foreshadowed Head Start programs for impoverished preschoolers and early intervention programs for children with developmental delays.

During the 1930s and early 1940s, FDR was sending the world a message: a physical handicap need not be a stigma. Roosevelt's example has been cited as a motivating force behind Pearl Buck's ultimate decision to tell the world about Carol. What FDR did for people with physical handicaps, she hoped to do for those with mental handicaps. Her decision to write *The Child Who Never Grew* was not motivated by confessional soul-baring. She had a greater goal: she wanted Carol's story to help others. Ms. Buck believed that Carol's life could be "of use in her generation," that her story "must be of use to human beings . . . her life must count."

In the 1950s, some medical and social advances were made to enhance the lives of people with mental retardation. For example, the etiology of phenylketonuria (PKU), a congenital disease resulting in metal retardation, was found to be the inability to metabolize an essential amino acid. Once PKU's cause was discovered, testing and dietary treatment became available soon after birth. In 1959, three French scientists discovered the cause of Down syndrome: a genetic mishap near the time of conception caused an extra chromosome in every cell of the body. Such scientific information helped parents to understand that they were not at fault. Nature is imperfect. Prior to these medical discoveries, many parents typically believed that they could have prevented their child's mental retardation. A former teacher of mine, for example, thought that a minor automobile accident when she was pregnant had caused her son to be born with Down syndrome. We know today that many forms of mental retardation result from genetic accidents or other unforeseen causes, but also that others do have environmental causes such as substance abuse during pregnancy.

While the 1950s and 1960s brought certain advances, it was often a dance of three steps forward and two steps backward. Across the country, many state institutions sprung up or expanded, warehousing thousands of mentally retarded persons in huge facilities. Had Ms. Buck's writing career not been so successful and she had been unable to afford a private institution for her daughter, Carol might have resided at a mammoth public institution called Pennhurst in eastern Pennsylvania, not far from where Pearl Buck moved after leaving China permanently. In 1950, Pennhurst housed 2,600 persons. Established in 1908 for 500 residents, Pennhurst at its most crowded was home to 3,200 people. After a thirteen-year landmark lawsuit, it was closed in 1987 and its residents were moved to small group homes.

Although institutions thrived through the 1950s and 1960s, a greater public acceptance of people with mental retardation slowly began to grow. The National Association for Retardation Children was founded in 1950 to lobby legislators and improve public awareness. (The organization later changed its name to the Association for Retarded Citizens and again in 1991 to "The ARC" because it maintains that the word "retarded" carries a stigma.) In 1954, a "Creed for Exceptional Children" was proclaimed at a U.S. Office of Education Conference on Qualification and Preparation of Teachers. The driving force behind these efforts were parents, parents like Ms. Buck who wanted a better life for their children and those who would be born with similar problems in the future.

Pearl Buck was a strong supporter of parents. She wrote many letters of encouragement, including one in 1952 to a mother who was organizing other parents on behalf of their children: ". . . The primary problem of parents such as we are is to awaken the public to the rights that retarded children have. It is a strange thing that in our great friendly democracy these little retarded children . . . receive no attention and little help of any kind from state or community. Yet many of the children could be aided to became useful citizens if they had special training and could work in a protected environment. . . . I am deeply interested in such groups as yours, for it is the parents of retarded children who must awaken our people. . . . The parents must stir up the community not only to give these children every opportunity for life, but also to treat them as human beings."

Another milestone for people with mental retardation was the Kennedy family's revelation that they had a sister who was mentally retarded. Rosemary Kennedy was born two years before Carol Buck. Like Pearl Buck, the Kennedys struggled for years with Rosemary's delayed development. Denial gradually gave way to acknowledgment. Family friend and presidential speechwriter Theodore C. Sorensen has written that President John F. Kennedy was very sensitive to press stories about Rosemary "until the whole family decided that a more matter-of-fact attitude better served the fight against mental retardation."

JFK then threw the power and leadership of the Presidency behind the budding movement to improve the lives of mentally retarded people when he declared in 1963, "Although retarded children may be the victim of fate, they will not be the victims of our neglect." Another sister, Eunice Kennedy Shriver, established Special Olympics in 1968, which has become an international program of athletic competition and physical fitness for children and adults who are retarded. The family also set up the Joseph P. Kennedy Jr. Foundation, which sponsors other programs.

As U.S. Attorney General in 1963, Robert F. Kennedy told a Congressional committee: "We visited a state hospital for the mentally retarded on a bright April day when you would have expected all the children to be playing outside. The children were inside, standing in a room which was bare but for a few benches. The floor was covered with urine. Severely retarded patients were left naked in cubicles, which suggested kennels. . . . Patients were washed by a device resembling a car wash. . . . The only toilets for the approximately seventy patients in a large ward were located in the middle of the room, permitting no privacy. The hospital's hard-working but inadequate staff could provide at best only custodial care."

Not all residential institutions were so inhumane, but institutionalization was the order of the day in the 1960s. Buildings were expanding to meet demand—each institution for the retarded averaged 340 people waiting for admission, as Ms. Buck wrote in her 1965 book, *The Gifts They Bring* (written with Gweneth Zarfoss about the positive potential of people with mental retardation).

For those who remained at home with their families, public schools provided little more than babysitting service. The "special ed kids" were isolated in classrooms of their own, or even in separate school buildings, away from their brothers, sisters, and neighbors. Many public schools refused to enroll children who were mentally retarded when they reached the usual age for kindergarten or first grade because they were considered "not ready" for school until they were older. After school age, some communities offered sheltered workshops where retarded adults worked alongside other retarded adults, assembly-line fashion, routinely sorting silverware, stuffing envelopes, or packing boxes of widgets.

The 1970s heralded a public outcry about inhumane conditions at large institutions like the one visited by Robert

Kennedy. The demand for better treatment reached a crescendo and drove the "deinstitutionalization" movement. Institutions like New York's Willowbrook received such media attention that scandalous living conditions could no longer be ignored. By the end of the decade, fewer than four percent of Americans with mental retardation lived in institutions.

At the same time, parents of young children with mental retardation began to look around at institutions, public schools, and sheltered workshops. "Our children should not be doomed to a lifetime in an institution," parents protested. "They deserve better than that! . . . And why do they have to stay home from public school until they are nine or ten when we're paying taxes for all our other children to begin school at age five? . . . Can't they do more than sort silverware in a workshop all day?"

Just as the 1960s and 1970s launched the expansion of rights for minorities and women, the rights of people with mental retardation would become recognized and secured in the law. But unlike minorities and women, most people with retardation needed advocates to speak on their behalf. Innovative educational programs resulted from parents banding together and confronting legislatures and service providers. Early intervention (or infant stimulation) programs for developmentally delayed babies began in the early 1970s largely because parents demanded that their children receive a head start on their education. Few had heard of Skeele and Dye's earlier work, but most knew that if federal Head Start programs were helping economically deprived children, the same early start could benefit their preschoolers as well.

Historic legislation was passed in 1973 and 1975 to correct past injustices. The first was Section 504 of the Rehabilitation Act of 1973, which prohibited discrimination against handicapped persons in federally funded programs and protected rights to education and to participate fully in community life. The Education for All Handicapped Children Act of 1975 (Public Law 94–142) guaranteed a free, appropriate education to every American child, regardless of handicap, an education "designed to meet their unique needs." The goal of this law was to provide children who have special needs with individualized educational plans, created jointly by parents and professionals. Children with disabilities were to be educated in the least restrictive environment—meaning that they were no longer to be segregated away from other children. The law also applied the right of due process (the constitutional right to a fair hearing by an impartial person) to all decisions about special education. Until this legislation, due process in schools had been ignored as children routinely were deprived of educational services, expelled from school without explanation, or labelled "ineducable."

Richard Nixon declared a national goal of reducing by half the incidence of mental retardation by the end of the twentieth century. But setting goals and passing laws mean little unless they are backed up by a commitment of funds and will, as parents quickly learned. Without adequate funding, improved educational opportunities guaranteed by PL 94–142 were empty promises. As the 1970s became the 1980s, parents again had to become a driving force—writing to legislators, speaking before school boards, occasionally marching peacefully with their children in tow—to see that educational programs for the mentally retarded were funded.

Four months after the 1981 inauguration, the Reagan administration announced its intention to repeal PL 94–142. That misguided effort failed, but the administration attempted in 1982 to weaken the law by issuing restrictive regulations (to allow states and local school systems to set their own schedules for implementing "free and appropriate education"; to diminish parental participation in educational planning; to remove handicapped children from classroom on the basis of their being "disruptive"; and to reduce health-related special services).

After fighting so long and hard for the enactment of PL 94–142, parents and educators were not about to sit back and let it be gutted. Washington received thousands of letters and phone calls from angry parents and professionals. This outpouring of protest forced Reagan's Secretary of Education, Terrel H. Bell, to withdraw most of the proposed changes. But throughout the rest of the 1980s, the Federal government footed only a small portion of the total special education bill, leaving individual states and localities to respond in patchwork fashion. The irony was that, by the 1980s, educational researchers had clearly demonstrated the value of mainstreaming students. The Educational Testing Service of Princeton, for example, conducted a three-year study which showed that both handicapped and non-handicapped students benefit from integrated school settings.

Another piece of landmark legislation was the Americans with Disabilities Act of 1990. Like its predecessors, its net effect will depend on commitment and dollars. The law is not backed by Federal money, but private businesses must make a good faith effort to bring down barriers and make workplaces more accessible to disabled individuals. Some business leaders initially cried that following the letter of the law would be prohibitively expensive for them, but most are finding that not to be true. And many business people have come to realize that workers with physical and mental disabilities are often more reliable employees who cause less turnover than others.

Since the mid-1980s, the concept of "supported employment" has begun to grow. Adults with mental retardation are assigned "job coaches" who help them find a job and learn the precise skills to hold it. Once the worker learns the ropes, the job coach steps back and moves on, leaving the worker responsible to the employer. A number of major businesses (Marriott, Pizza Hut, McDonald's, Boeing, United Airlines, and IBM, to name a few) have hired thousands of mentally retarded employees through supported employment program. In one instance, Pizza Hut hired 1,012 disabled workers (73 percent of whom were mentally retarded) and found that they stayed four to five times longer in the job than non-disabled workers. This lower turnover saved Pizza Hut over $2.2 million in recruiting, hiring, and training new employees.

Much progress has been made in recent years: Causes of mental retardation are better understood and, in some instances, preventable. Improved medical care insures a healthier, longer life. Babies and toddlers are receiving early intervention to enhance their cognitive and physical abilities. School-age children are enrolled in classes alongside non-disabled students, with special support services provided when necessary. Teenagers and young adults are learning job-related skills and participating in scout troops, swim teams, and other recreational activities. Adults are living in group homes and apartments, shopping, bowling, going to the movies, riding public transportation, working in their communities, and paying taxes.

Public understanding of mental retardation has also grown, thanks in large part to enlightened leaders in the media. An early breakthrough occurred in the late 1970s when *Sesame Street* included mentally retarded and physically disabled children in a regular weekly segment. One of those children, Jason Kingsley, went on to act in an episode of *The Fall Guy*, a television series starring Lee Majors. And a made-for-TV movie was filmed about Jason's life. More recently, the ABC network series, *Life Goes On*, features as one of its stars Christopher Burke, a young man who has Down syndrome. Other television programs—including *L.A. Law* and *Kate and Allie*—have used non-disabled actors to portray adult characters with mental retardation. Children with obvious handicaps are now beginning to appear as models in advertisements for children's clothing and toys.

How might Pearl Buck look upon these developments? As both the parent and humanitarian she was, Ms. Buck would undoubtedly be heartened by the overall progress in wider acceptance and opportunity. Although Carol lived all but nine years of her life in an institution, Pearl Buck was not an apologist for institutionalization. She knew that retarded children had great gifts to offer, including the "intangible quality of love," as she wrote in *The Gifts They Bring*. She believed that those gifts should be spread around. In *The Gifts They Bring,* she foresaw the future when she described a community as an "enlarged family" enfolding not only the strong and able but "the weakest and most helpless" as well. She wrote, "And by providing the atmosphere in which he (the retarded child) can grow, we provide the atmosphere for all to grow. We do not believe in segregating the retarded child from other children. Let the normal child understand that all are not as fortunate as he. Let the normal child learn to be grateful that by chance it is he who is strong, and let him learn to use his strength for the less fortunate."

Pearl Buck lived long enough (until 1973) to witness the earliest dawn of integrated classes and deinstutionalization. Had Carol been born two generations later, Pearl Buck would surely have been on the front lines with parents who enrolled their preschoolers in early programs, pushed for mainstreaming in regular classrooms, demanded job training for their adolescents, and full citizenship for their young adults.

Individuals with mental retardation, their families, friends, and advocates, owe a great debt to Pearl Buck for her brave disclosure about Carol in 1950. Perhaps the biggest strides in human advancement are taken in small steps—one person to another. Perhaps racism is broken down in small steps, as three Asian, Afro-American, and white neighbors talk together on one's front porch. Perhaps homophobia is diminished a bit whenever one gay worker and one straight colleague become friends outside the office. Perhaps men understand women better when a father listens to his daughter describe her experience with sexual harassment. More than all the statistics, charts, and research data, personal stories that tell "the real truth," as my six-year-old niece says, can move mountains and change lives.

Personal stories. Telling and listening. Pearl Buck excelled in the telling. For those who listen, her story pushes the experience of mental retardation farther along—into a realm of better understanding, compassion, and dedication than had previously existed. And, if I may end on a personal note: I first read *The Child Who Never Grew* in 1974, shortly after my first child was born with Down syndrome. Although the book was then twenty-four years old and I recognized that some of it was a bit dated, I took great comfort in Pearl Buck's story. She knew my pain and I knew hers. She also gave me support and hope, as her words will continue to do for other families now and in the future.

The Child Who Never Grew

I have been a long time making up my mind to write this story. It is a true one, and that makes it hard to tell. Several reasons have helped me to reach the point this morning, after an hour or so of walking through the winter woods, when I have finally resolved that the time has come for the story to be told. Some of the reasons are in the many letters which I have received over the years from parents with a child like mine. They write to ask me what to do. When I answer I can only tell them what I have done. They ask two things of me: first, what they shall do for their children; and, second, how shall they bear the sorrow of having such a child?

The first question I can answer, but the second is difficult indeed, for endurance of inescapable sorrow is something which has to be learned alone. And only to endure is not enough. Endurance can be a harsh and bitter root in one's life, bearing poisonous and gloomy fruit, destroying other lives. Endurance is only the beginning. There must be acceptance and the knowledge that sorrow fully accepted brings its own gifts. For there is an alchemy in sorrow. It can be transmuted into wisdom, which, if it does not bring joy, can yet bring happiness.

The final reason for setting down this story is that I want my child's life to be of use in her generation. She is one who has never grown mentally beyond her early childhood, therefore she is forever a child, although in years she is old enough now to have been married and to have children of her own—my grandchildren who will never be.

The first cry from my heart, when I knew that she would never be anything but a child, was the age-old cry that we all make before inevitable sorrow: "Why must this happen to me?" To this there could be no answer and there was none. When I knew at last that there could never be an answer, my own resolve shaped into the determination to make meaning out of the meaningless, and so provide the answer, though it was of my own making. I resolved that my child, whose natural gifts were obviously unusual, even though they were never to find experience, was not to be wasted. If she could not make the contribution she should have made to her generation through her genius for music, if her healthy body was never to bear fruit, if her strong energies were not to be creatively used, then the very facts of her condition, her existence as it was and is today, must be of use to human beings. In one way, if not the other, her life must count. To know that it was not wasted might assuage what could not be prevented or cured.

This resolve did not come to me immediately. I grew toward it, but once I had reached it I have held to it through all the years of her life. I have let it work in quiet ways, dreading the cold eyes of the curious. Now, today, I will forget those whom I dread, who, after all, are very few. I will remember the many who are kind, who will understand my purpose in telling this story, who will want to help to fulfill this purpose because it is their purpose too.

I am always moved, with grateful wonder, by the goodness of people. For the few who are prying or meanly critical, for the very few who rejoice in the grief of others, there are the thousands who are kind. I have come to believe that the natural human heart is good, and I have observed that this goodness is found in all varieties of people, and that it can and does prevail in spite of other corruptions. This human goodness alone provides hope enough for the world.

I have sometimes wondered, as the years passed, whether the moment would come when I might feel that my purpose for my child must include the telling of her story. I dreaded this, and do dread it. Nevertheless, the time has come. For there is afoot in our country a great new movement to help all children like her. It is too late, of course, for her to be helped, but it is not too late for many little ones, and surely for others yet to be born. For we are beginning to understand the importance and the significance of the mentally retarded person in our human society. Almost one person in every hundred is or will be mentally retarded,* and of these the majority are retarded from non-inherited causes. The old stigma of "something in the family" is all too often unjust.

The total number of retarded children is not large in proportion to the whole population, and yet it is enough to cause trouble everywhere. Homes are unhappy, parents distraught, schoolrooms confused by the presence of these who for no fault of their own are as they are. As parents die or cannot care for them, as teachers give them up, these children drift helplessly into the world, creating havoc wherever they go. They become the tools of those more

---

* [Current estimates are that about three people in every hundred have mental retardation.]

clever; they are the hopeless juvenile delinquents; they fall
into criminal ways because they know not what they do.
And all they do is in innocence, for of God's many children
these are the most innocent.

⚘ I rejoice in the dawn of a better understanding of such
children, for the public attitude until now has been a sorely
⚘mistaken one. Parents have been bewildered and ashamed
when their child is backward, when he cannot learn in
school, when perhaps he cannot even learn to talk. It has
been a misfortune to be hidden. Neighbors whisper that
so-and-so's child is "not right." The family is taught to try
to pretend that poor Harry or Susie is only slow. The shame
of the parents infects all the children and sorrow spreads
its blight. The child himself, poor little one, feels, though
he cannot comprehend, his own inferiority. He lives in
surrounding gloom. His mother cannot smile when she
looks at him, and his father looks away at the sight of him.
In spite of their tender love for him—for the honor of the
human heart, it can passionately protect the helpless creature who is its cross—the child understands enough to know
that there is something unfortunate about him. His shadow
falls before him, wherever he goes.

Now, thank God, the shadow lifts. Wise men and
women are beginning to reason that it is only common sense
to accept the mentally retarded person as part of the human
family, and to educate him in the things he can do, so that
he may be happy in himself and useful to society. That this
may be done, the primary work of research must progress
as it never has. We must somehow discover why it is that
so many people do not develop mentally to their full

capacity. There must be remediable causes and certainly there are preventable causes. We know, for example, that if a women has German measles in the first three months of pregnancy, her child may be born mentally defective, but we do not know why. We must know why. The Mongoloid child can appear in any family. He is really an unfinished child and is usually a first or last child. We must find out what conditions in the mother cause this child.* It is not necessary that children be born never to grow to their fullest selves. The windows are opened, at last, upon this dark corner of human life and the light shines upon the children's faces and into the hearts of their parents.

That my child, therefore, may have some small share in creating this new light, I tell her story. She cannot know what she does, but I who am her mother will do it for her and in her name, that others like her may have the benefits of a fuller knowledge, a better understanding. It will not be easy to tell it all truthfully, but it is of no use to tell it otherwise. Perhaps when it is finished there will be comfort because it is told for a high purpose.

I must go back into the early years of my young womanhood—no, even before that. When I was a little girl

---

* ["Mongolism" was the accepted term for Down syndrome when *The Child Who Never Grew* was first published. Today it is known that the condition is caused by the presence of an extra twenty-first chromosome in a child's cells, although what causes that extra chromosome is not fully understood. We do know that early or late birth order does *not* predispose a child to Down syndrome, and that it can develop as the result of both maternal and paternal factors.]

myself, not more than seven years old, living in China, I had an awakening of the spirit. Until then I suppose I was the usual selfish creature, thinking of play and of nothing else except having my own way. I had few children to play with and one of my dear friends was a gay young American woman, who lived for a very short time next door to us. She was married, and during the few months she was our neighbor she had a baby girl born to her. It was my first experience of an American baby and of all the tender care that the average American baby gets.

Every morning I was the attendant at the bath. I poured the water and warmed the towel and handed the mother the little garments, one by one. I was allowed a moment of my own, when the fair-haired blue-eyed little baby, smelling sweetly of soap and freshness, was put into my arms. That was the height of the day for me. I can remember even now, even after I have held so many babies in my arms, babies of many colors and races, the joy of that first little one. I might have grieved very much when the transient neighbors went their way, had not my own little sister been born, fortunately, that same spring in the heart of the vast old city on the Yangtze River which was then my home. I busied myself mightily about our own baby. My mother was desperately ill after the birth, and the chief care of the baby fell upon our old Chinese amah and me. I was so happy I did not know how near my mother was to death.

I have begun this story so long ago because I can see now that I loved my child long before she was born. I wanted children of my own, as most woman do, but I think my intense love of life added depth to natural longing.

Something certainly I learned from the Chinese, who value children above all else in life. The Chinese love children for their own sakes and beyond. Children mean the continuity of human life, and human life is wonderful and precious. I absorbed the atmosphere in which I was reared.

My child was born in the height of my young womanhood. I was full of strength and vigor and the enjoyment of life. My life lay in places which might seem strange to my fellow Americans but which were not strange to me. My home then was outside a small mud-walled town in North China. From my windows I looked over miles of flat farm land, green with wheat and sorghum in the summer, and in the winter the color of dust. Springtimes were loveliest, for above the young green wheat mirages shimmered. We had neither lakes nor mountains near, but the mirages brought them to us. They hung like fantastic dreams above the horizon. It was difficult to believe that they were not real.

Like every young woman, I had many dreams. There were books that I wanted to write when I had lived enough to know life. Life I had always wanted in plenty and overflowing, and I think, looking back, that I always ran to meet it. Certainly I always wanted children. So when I knew my first child was to be born, one year in the spring, my joy rose to the height of my dreams. I did not know then that there was to be only one. I did not think of such a possibility. Everything had always gone well with me, all my life. I was one of the fortunately born. I took good fortune for granted. I saw my house full of children.

I remember so well the first time my little girl and I saw each other. It was a warm mild morning in March. A Chinese friend had brought me a pot of budding plum blossoms the day before, and a spray of them had opened. That was the first thing I saw when I came out of the ether. The next thing was my baby's face. The young Chinese nurse had wrapped her in a pink blanket and she held her up for me to see. Mine was a pretty baby, unusually so. Her features were clear, her eyes even then, it seemed to me, wise and calm. She looked at me and I at her with mutual comprehension and I laughed.

I remember I said to the nurse, "Doesn't she look very wise for her age?" She was then less than an hour old.

"She does, indeed," the nurse declared. "And she is beautiful too. There is a special purpose for this child."

How often have I thought of those words! I thought of them proudly at first, as the child grew, always healthy, always good. I remember when she was two months old that an old friend saw her the first time. The child had never seen a man with a black mustache before and she stared for a moment and then drew down her little mouth to weep, though some pride kept her from actual tears.

"Extraordinary," my friend said, "She knows already what is strange to her."

I remember when she was only a month older that she lay in her little basket upon the sun deck of a ship. I had taken her there for the morning air as we traveled. The people who promenaded upon the deck stopped often to look at her, and my pride grew as they spoke of her unusual beauty and of the intelligence of her deep blue eyes.

I do not know where or at what moment the growth of her intelligence stopped, nor to this day do we know why it did. There was nothing in my family to make me fear that my child might be one of those who do not grow. Indeed, I was fortunate in my own ancestry on both sides. My father's family was distinguished for achievement in languages and letters, and my mother's family was a cultivated one. On her father's side my child had a sturdy ancestry, which had occasionally produced persons of distinction. I had no fears of any sort—indeed, I was almost too innocent of fear. I had seen in my youth only one defective child, the little son of a missionary, and he had made no impression on me beyond one of love and pity. Of Chinese children of the sort I had seen none. There seem to be few, and such as there are remain at home, carefully tended. Perhaps, too, they die young. At any rate, no young mother could have been less prepared than I for what was to come.

My little daughter's body continued its healthy progress. We had left North China by then, and were living in Nanking, which, next to Peking, perhaps, is China's richest city in history and humanity. Though my home was inside the city walls, it was still country living. Our house was surrounded by lawn and gardens, a bamboo grove and great trees. When the city walls were built, centuries ago, enough land was enclosed so that if the city were besieged, the people would not starve. Our compound was surrounded by farms and fish ponds.

It was a pleasant and healthy home for a child. She was still beautiful, as she would be to this day were the light of the mind behind her features. I think I was the last to perceive that something was wrong. She was my first child, and I had no close comparison to make with others. She was three years old when I first began to wonder.

For at three she did not yet talk. Now that my adopted babies have taught me so much, I realize that speech comes as naturally to the normal child as breathing. He does not need to be taught to talk—he talks as he grows. He hears words without knowing it and day by day increases the means of conveying his widening thoughts. Still, I became uneasy. In the midst of my pleasant surroundings, in all the fresh interest of a new period in Chinese history when the Nationalist government was setting itself up with such promise, I found life exciting and good. Yet I can remember my growing uneasiness about my child. She looked so well, her cheeks pink, her hair straight and blond, her eyes the clear blue of health. Why then did speech delay!

I remember asking friends about their children, and voicing my new anxiety about my child. Their replies were comforting, too comforting. They told me that children talked at different ages, that a child growing up in the house with other children learned more quickly than an only child. They spoke all the empty words of assurance that friends, meaning well, will use, and I believed them. Afterward, when I knew the whole tragic truth, I asked them if they had no knowledge then of what had befallen my child. I found that they did have, that they had guessed and surmised and that the older ones even knew, but that they shrank from telling me.

To this day I cannot understand their shrinking. For to me truth is so much dearer than any comforting falsehood, so much kinder in its clean-cutting edge than fencing and evasion, that the better a friend is the more he must use truth. There is value in the quick and necessary wound. Thus my child was nearly four years old before I discovered for myself that her mind had stopped growing. To all of us there comes the hour of awakening to sad truth. Sometimes the whole awakening comes at once and in a moment. To others, like myself, it came in parts slowly. I was reluctant and unbelieving until the last.

It began one summer at a seashore in China, where the waves come in gently even in time of storm. It had been a mild and pleasant summer, shore set against mountains. I spent the mornings with my child on the beach and in the afternoons sometimes we went riding along the valleys on the small gray donkeys which stood for hire at the edge of the beach.

The child had now begun to talk, only a little, but still enough to quiet my fears for the moment. It must be remembered that I was wholly inexperienced in such children. Now my eyes can find in any crowd the child like mine. I see him first of all and then I see the mother, trying to smile, trying to speak to the child gaily, her gaiety a screen to hide him from the others. But then I did not see even my own child as she really was, I read meaning into her gestures and into the few broken words. "She doesn't talk because she gets everything she wants without it," a friend complained. So I tried to teach my child to ask for a thing first. She seemed not to understand.

I must have been more anxious than I knew, however, for I remember I went one day to hear an American visiting

pediatrician give a lecture on the preschool child, and as I
listened to her I realized that something was very wrong
indeed with my child. The doctor pointed out signs of
danger which I had not understood. The slowness to walk,
the slowness to talk, and then when the child could walk,
the increasing restlessness which took the form of constant
running hither and thither, were all danger signs. What I
had taken to be the vitality of a splendid body I saw now
might be the super energy of a mind that had not kept
control of the body.

After the meeting was over, I remember, I asked the
doctor to come and see my child. She promised to come the
next day. I told no one of my growing fear and through that
sleepless night I went over and over in my mind all the good
signs, the things the child could do: that she could feed
herself; that she could put on her clothes, though not fasten
buttons; that she liked to look at picture books; that she
understood so much more than she could say. But I did not
want false comfort. I wanted now and quickly the whole
truth.

The doctor came the next day and sat a long time
watching my child, and then she shook her head, "Something is wrong," she said, "I do not know what it is. You
must have a consultation of doctors. Let them tell you, if
they know."

She pointed out to me the danger signs I had not seen,
or would not see. The child's span of attention was very
short indeed, far shorter than it should have been at her
age. Much of her fleet light running had no purpose—it was
merely motion. Her eyes, so pure in their blue, were blank

when one gazed into their depths. They did not hold or respond. They were changeless. Something was very wrong.

I thanked her and she went away. Thinking it over, I saw there was no reason why a stranger should stay to tell me more. Perhaps she knew no more. There is no task more difficult than to tell a parent that the beloved child will never grow to be an adult. I have done it sometimes since, and I have not allowed myself to shrink from it, but it has been hard. The heart can break more than once.

The doctors met the next day. I can still see the scene as though it took place before my eyes now. The house had a wide veranda, facing the sea. It was a glorious morning, and the sea was violet blue and calm except for the gentle white surf at the coast. The child had been with her Chinese nurse playing on the sand and wading in the water. I called and they came up the path between the bamboos. In spite of my terror, I was proud of my child as she stood before the doctors. She had on a little white swimming suit and her firm sun-browned body was strong and beautiful. In one hand she held her pail and shovel and in the other a white shell.

"She looks well enough," one of the doctors murmured.

Then they began to ask questions. I answered them with all the honesty I had. Nothing but honesty would do now. As they listened they watched and they began to see. The shell dropped from her hand and she did not pick it up. Her head drooped. The oldest doctor, who had known my parents, lifted her to his knee and began to test her reflexes. They were weak—almost nonexistent.

The doctors were kind men and I begged them to tell me what they thought and then tell me what to do. I think they were honest in their wish to do this. But they did not know what was wrong or, whatever was wrong, how to cure it. I sat in silence and watched the child. I began to feel that they were agreed that development had stopped in the child, but did not know why. There were so few physical symptoms—only the ones I have mentioned. They plied me with questions about the child's past, about her illnesses: had she ever had a high temperature, had she ever had a fall? There had been nothing. She had been sound from her birth and so cared for that she had never been hurt.

"You must take her to America," they told me at last. "There the doctors may know what is wrong. We can only say there is something wrong."

Then began that long journey which parents of such children know so well. I have talked with many of them since and it is always the same. Driven by the conviction that there must be someone who can cure, we take our children over the surface of the whole earth, seeking the one who can heal. We spend all the money we have and we borrow until there is no one else to lend. We go to doctors good and bad, to anyone, for only a wisp of hope. We are gouged by unscrupulous men who make money from our terror, but now and again we meet those saints who, seeing the terror and guessing the empty purse, will take nothing for their advice, since they cannot heal.

So I came and went, too, over the surface of the earth, gradually losing hope and yet never quite losing it, for no doctor said firmly that the child could never be healed.

There were always the last hesitant words, "I don't want to say it is hopeless"; and so I kept hoping, in the way parents have.

It was getting harder all the time for another reason. The child was older and bigger and her broken speech and babyish ways were conspicuous. I had no sense of shame for myself. I had grown up among the Chinese, who take any human infirmity for what it is. Blind people, the lame, the halt, the tongue-tied, the deformed—during my life in China I had seen that all came and went among others and were accepted for themselves. Their infirmities were not ignored. Sometimes they were even made the cause of nicknames.

For example, Little Cripple was a playmate of my own early childhood, a boy with a twisted leg. According to our western notions, it would have been cruel to call him by his deformity. But the Chinese did not mean it so. That was the way he was, literally, and his twisted leg was part of himself. There was some sort of catharsis even for the boy in this taking for granted an affliction. Somehow it was easier than the careful ignoring of my American friends. The sufferer did not feel any need to hide himself. There he was, as he was, and everybody knew him. It was better than any sweet pretending that he was like everybody else.

More than this, the Chinese believed that since Heaven ordains, it was a person's fate to be whatever he was and it was neither his fault nor his family's. They believed, too, with a sort of human tenderness, that if a person were handicapped in one way, there were compensations, also provided by Heaven. Thus a blind person was always treated with respect and even sometimes with fear, for it was thought he had a perception far beyond mere seeing.

All the years my child and I had lived among the Chinese we had breathed this frank atmosphere. My Chinese friends discussed my child with me easily as they discussed their own. But they were not experienced enough to know what was wrong or even that it was wrong. "The eyes of her wisdom are not yet opened," was the way they put it. "For some persons wisdom comes early and for others late—be patient." This was what they told me. When we walked on the narrow winding streets of our old city no one noticed when she stopped reasonlessly to clap her hands or if, without reason, she began to dance. Yes, the Chinese were kind to my child and to me. If they did notice her, it was only to smile at what they took to be her pleasure, and they laughed with her.

It was on the streets of Shanghai that I first learned that people were not all so kind. Two young American women walked along the street, newcomers from my own country, I suppose, by their smart garments. They stared at my child and when we had passed one of them said to the other, "The kid is nuts." It was the first time I had ever heard the slang phrase and I did not know what it meant. I had to ask someone before I knew. Truth can be put into brutal words. From that day I began to shield my child.

There is no use in giving the details of the long, sorrowful journey. We crossed the sea and we went everywhere, to child clinics, to gland specialists, to psychologists. I know now that it was all no use. There was no hope from the first—there never had been any. I do not blame those men and women for not telling me so—not altogether. I suppose some of them knew, but perhaps they didn't. At any rate, the end of each conference was to send us on to someone else, perhaps a thousand miles away.

One famous gland specialist gave me considerable hope, and we undertook a year-long treatment with dosages of gland medicine. It did my child no good, and yet I do not regret it, for from what I learned that year I was able to save another child who really needed the treatment a few years later. I saw a little boy who at four was still crawling on his hands and knees and I recognized in his symptoms— the dry skin and hair, the pallid flesh, the big ungainly weak body, the retarded mind—the need for thyroid treatment. I did not know his mother very well, but remembering the silence of my friends, I went to her and told her what I thought. There was a long moment when her flushed face showed me her inner struggle. She did not want to know— and yet she knew she must know. I went away, but after- ward she did take the child to the gland specialist and he was able to help the boy become normal. That boy was not really mentally retarded. He was suffering from a thyroid deficiency. Years later the mother and I met on different soil and she thanked me for that past day. But it took courage to speak. It always does.

The end of the journey for my child and me came one winter's day in Rochester, Minnesota. We had been sent finally to the Mayo Clinic, and day after day we had spent in the endless and meticulous detail of complete examina- tion. My confidence had grown as the process went on.

Surely so much study, so much knowledge, would tell me the truth and what to do with it.

We went at last into the office of the head of the children's department. It was evening and almost everybody had gone home. The big building was silent and empty. Outside the window I saw only darkness. My little girl was very tired and I remember she leaned her head against me and began to cry silently, and I took her upon my lap and held her close while I listened. The doctor was kind and good. I can see him still, a tall, rather young man, his eyes gentle and his manner slow as though he did not want anyone to be hurried or anxious. He held in his hand the reports sent in from all the departments where my child had been examined, and he made his diagnosis. Much of it was good. All the physical parts were excellent. My child had been born with a fine body.

There were other things good too. She had certain remarkable abilities, especially in music. There were signs of an unusual personality struggling against some sort of handicap. But—the mind was severely retarded.

I asked the question that I asked now every day of my life: "Why?"

He shook his head. "I don't know. Somewhere along the way, before birth or after, growth stopped."

He did not hurry me, and I sat on, still holding the child. Any parent who has been through such an hour knows that monstrous ache of the heart which becomes physical and permeates muscle and bone.

"Is it hopeless?" I asked him.

Kind man, he could not bear to say that it was. Perhaps he was not really sure. At least he would not say he was sure. "I think I would not give up trying," was what he finally said.

That was all. He was anxious to get home and there was no more reason to stay. He had done all he could. So again my child and I went out of the doctor's office and walked down the wide empty hall. The day was over and I had to think what to do next.

Now came the moment for which I shall be grateful as long as I live. I suppose to be told that my child could be well would have meant a gratitude still higher; but that being impossible, I have to thank a man who came quietly out of an empty room as I passed. He was a small, inconspicuous person, spectacled, a German by looks and accent. I had seen him in the head doctor's office once or twice. He had, in fact, brought in the sheaf of reports and then had gone away without speaking. I had seen him but without attention, although now I recognized him.

He came out almost stealthily and beckoned to me to follow him into the empty room. I went in, half bewildered, my child clinging to my hand. He began to speak quickly in his broken English, his voice almost harsh, his eyes sternly upon mine.

"Did he tell you the child might be cured?" he demanded.

"He—he didn't say she could not," I stammered.

"Listen to what I tell you!" he commanded. "I tell you, madame, the child can never be normal. Do not deceive yourself. You will wear out your life and beggar your family unless you give up hope and face the truth. She will never be well—do you hear me? I know—I have seen these children. Americans are all too soft. I am not soft. It is better to be hard, so that you can know what to do. This child will be a burden on you all your life. Get ready to bear that burden. She will never be able to speak properly. She will never be able to read or write, she will never be more than about four years old, at best. Prepare yourself, madame! Above all, do not let her absorb you. Find a place where she can be happy and leave her there and live your own life. I tell you the truth for your own sake."

I can remember these words exactly as he spoke them. I suppose the shock photographed them upon my memory. I remember, too, exactly how he looked, a little man, shorter than I, his face pale, a small, clipped black mustache under which his lips were grim. He looked cruel, but I know he was not. I know now that he suffered while he spoke. He believed in the truth.

I don't know what I said or even if I said anything. I remember walking down the endless hall again alone with the child. I cannot describe my feelings. Anyone who has been through such moments will know, and those who have not cannot know, whatever words I might use. Perhaps the best way to put it is that I felt as though I were bleeding inwardly and desperately. The child, glad to be free, began capering and dancing, and when she saw my face twisted with weeping, she laughed.

It was all a long time ago and yet it will never be over as long as I live. That hour is with me still.

I did not stop trying, of course, in spite of what the little German had said, but I think I knew in my heart from that moment on that he was right and that there was no hope. I was able to accept the final verdict when it came because I had already accepted it before, though unconsciously, and I took my child home again to China. I shall forever be grateful to him, whose name I do not even know. He cut the wound deep, but it was clean and quick. I was brought at once face to face with the inevitable.

II

*W*hat I am writing is no unique experience. It is one common to many parents. Every retarded child means a stricken, heartsick family. I meet often nowadays with parents' organizations, parents of mentally deficient children who are coming together in their deep need for mutual comfort and support. Most of them are young people and how my heart aches for them! I know every step of their road to Calvary.

"The schools won't take our children," one of them said to me the other day. "The neighbors don't want them around. The other children are mean to them. What shall we do? Where can we go? Our child is still a human being. He is still an American citizen. He has some rights, hasn't he? So have we, haven't we? It's not a crime to have a child like ours."

No, it is not a crime, but people—teachers in schools, neighbors—can behave as though it were. You who have had a mentally deficient child know all that I mean.

When the inevitable knowledge was forced upon me that my child would never be as other children are, I found myself with two problems, both, it seemed to me, intolerable. The first was the question of her future. How does one safeguard a child who may live to be physically very old and will always be helpless? Her life would in all likelihood outlast my own. We come of long-lived stock, and though I might live to be old myself, I was borne down by grief and she had no burdens on her happy, childish mind. Worry and anxiety would never touch her. What if she lived to be even older than I? Who would care for her then? Yet there was a strange comfort in her happiness. As I watched her at play, myself so sorrowful, it came to me that this child would pass through life as the angels live in Heaven. The difficulties of existence would never be hers. She would not know that she was different from other children. The joys and irresponsibilities of childhood would be hers forever. My task was only to guarantee her safety, food and shelter—and kindness.

Yes, I have learned as the years passed to be intensely grateful for the fact that my child has no knowledge of herself. If it had to be that she could not be a fully developed human being, then I am glad she has remained a real child. The pitiful ones are those who know dimly that they are not as others are. I have seen them, too, and have heard them say humbly, "I know I'm dumb," or, "I know I'm nuts," or "I can't never git married because I'm queer." They do not fully understand even what they say, poor children, but they know enough to suffer.

Thank God my child has not been one of these! She has been able to enjoy sunshine and rain, she loves to skate and ride a tricycle, she finds pleasure in dolls and toy dishes and a sand pile. She likes to run on a beach and play in the waves. Above all is her never-failing joy in music. She finds her calm and resource in listening, hour after hour, to her records. The gift that is hidden in her shows itself in the still ecstasy with which she listens to the great symphonies, her lips smiling, her eyes gazing off into what distance I do not know.

She has her preferences for certain kinds of music. Church music, especially hymns, make her weep, and she cannot listen to them. I know how she feels. There is something infinitely pathetic in that chorus of wavering human voices raised to the God in Whom, not seeing, they must needs trust. She dislikes intensely all crooning and cheap rhythms, and in general popular music of all sorts. If someone puts on a jazz record, she seems in an agony. "No, no," she will say. "I don't like it." It must be taken not only from the phonograph, but away out of the room. But she will listen to all the great old music with endless delight. When she was at home this last summer she heard Beethoven's Fifth Symphony through entirely, sitting motionless beside the instrument. When it was finished she wanted it all over again. Her taste is unerring. By some instinct, too, she knows each one of her own large collection of records. I do not know how, since she cannot read, but she can distinguish each record from the others and will search until she finds the one that suits her mood.

I put this down because it is one of the compensations, and parents of other children like her ought to know that there are such compensations. These little children find their joys. I know one little boy—I say "little," and yet he is a grown man in body—who gets creative pleasure from his collection of brightly colored rags. He sorts them over and over again, rejoicing in their hues and textures. He is never wearied of them. The parent learns to be grateful that pleasure finds its expression, if not in ways that benefit the world, at least in ways that satisfy and enrich the child. Quantitatively, of course, there is a difference between the bright rags and a box of paints that an artist uses. But qualitatively the two are the same to the boy and to the artist. Both find the same spiritual satisfaction.

To parents I say first that if you discover that your child cannot be normal, be glad he is below the possibility of knowing his own condition. The burden of life has been removed from him and it rests only upon you, who can learn how to bear it.

To learn how to bear the inevitable sorrow is not easily done. I can look back on it now, the lesson learned, and see the steps; but when I was taking them they were hard indeed, each apparently insurmountable. For in addition to the practical problem of how to protect the child's life, which may last beyond the parent's, there is the problem of one's own self in misery. All the brightness of life is gone, all the pride in parenthood. There is more than pride gone, there is an actual sense of one's life being cut off in the child. The stream of the generations is stopped. Death would be far easier to bear, for death is final. What was is no more. How often did I cry out in my heart that it would be better if my child died! If that shocks you who have not known, it will not shock those who do know. I would have welcomed death for my child and would still welcome it, for then she would be finally safe.

It is inevitable that one ponders much on this matter of a kindly death. Every now and again I see in the newspapers the report of a man or woman who has put to death a mentally defective child. My heart goes out to such a one. I understand the love and despair which prompted the act. There is not only the despair that descends when the inevitable makes itself known, but there is the increasing despair of every day. For each day that makes clear that the child is only as he was yesterday drives the despair deeper, and there are besides the difficulties of care for such a child, the endless round of duties that seem to bear no fruit, tending a body that will be no more than a body however long it lives, gazing into the dull eyes that respond with no lively look, helping the fumbling hands—all these drive deeper the despair. And added to the despair is the terror and the question, "Who will do this in case I do not live?"

And yet I know that the parents of whom I read do wrong when they take to themselves a right which is not theirs and end the physical lives of their children. In love they may do it, and yet it is wrong. There is a sacred quality of life which none of us can fathom. All peoples feel it, for in all societies it is considered a sin for one human being to kill another for a reason of his own. Society decrees death for certain crimes, but the innocent may not be killed, and there is none more innocent than these children who never grow up. Murder remains murder. Were the right to kill a child put into a parent's hands, the effect would be evil indeed in our world. Were the right to kill any innocent person assumed by society, the effect would be monstrous. For first it might be only the helpless children who were killed, but then it might seem right to kill the helpless old; and then the conscience would become so dulled that prejudice would give the right to kill, and persons of a certain color or creed might be destroyed. The only safety is to reject completely the possibility of death as a means of ending any innocent life, however useless. The damage is not to the one who is killed, but to the one who kills. Euthanasia is a long, smooth-sounding word, and it conceals its danger as long smooth words do, but the danger is there, nevertheless.

It would be evasion, however, if I pretended that it was easy to accept the inevitable. For the sake of others who are walking that stony road, I will say that my inner rebellion lasted for many years. My common sense, my convictions of duty, all told me that I must not let the disaster spoil my own life or those of relatives and friends. But common sense and duty cannot always prevail when the heart is broken. My compromise was to learn to act on the surface as much like my usual self as possible, to talk, to laugh, to seem to take an interest in what went on. Underneath the rebellion burned, and tears flowed the moment I was alone. This surface acting kept me, of course, from having any real contact with other people. Doubtless they felt the surface bright and shallow, and were perhaps repelled by something hard and cold beneath which they could not reach. Yet it was necessary to maintain the surface, for it was my own protection, too. It was not possible to share with anyone in those years my inner state.

I can speak with detachment of it now, for it is over. I have learned my lesson. But it is interesting to me and may be of some small importance to some, merely as a process, to speak of learning how to live with sorrow that cannot be removed. Let me speak of it so, then.

The first phase of this process was disastrous and disorganizing. As I said, there was no more joy left in anything. All human relationships became meaningless.

Everything became meaningless. I took no more pleasure in the things I had enjoyed before; landscapes, flowers, music were empty. Indeed, I could not bear to hear music at all. It was years before I could listen to music. Even after the learning process had gone very far, and my spirit had become nearly reconciled through understanding, I could not hear music. I did my work during this time: I saw that my house was neat and clean, I cut flowers for the vases, I planned the gardens and tended my roses, and arranged for meals to be properly served. We had guests and I did my duty in the community. But none of it meant anything. My hands performed their routine. The hours when I really lived were when I was alone with my child. When I was safely alone I could let sorrow have its way, and in utter rebellion against fate my spirit spent its energy. Yet I tried to conceal my weeping from my child because she stared at me and laughed. It was this uncomprehending laughter which always and finally crushed my heart.

I do not know when the turn came, nor why. It came somehow out of myself. People were kind enough, but no help came from anyone. Perhaps that was my own fault. Perhaps I made my surface too smooth and natural so that no one could see beneath it. Partly that, perhaps, and partly it was, too, because people shrink from penetrating surfaces. Only those who know inescapable sorrow know what I mean.

It was in those days that I learned to distinguish between the two kinds of people in the world: those who have known inescapable sorrow and those who have not. For there are basically two kinds of sorrows: those which can be assuaged and those which cannot be. The death of parents is sad, for they cannot be replaced, but it is not inescapable sorrow. It is natural sorrow, that which one must expect in the normal course of life. The crippling of one's body, irremediably, is an inescapable sorrow. It has to be lived with; and more than that, it has to be used for some other sort of life than that planned in health. The sorrows which can be assuaged are those which life can cover and heal. Those which cannot be assuaged are those which change life itself and in a way themselves make life. Sorrows that can die can be assuaged, but living sorrow is never assuaged. It is a stone thrown into the stream, as Browning put it, and the water must divide itself and accommodate itself, for it cannot remove the stone.

I learned at last, merely by watching faces and by listening to voices, to know when I had found someone who knew what it was to live with sorrow that could not be ended. It was surprising and sad to discover how many such persons there were and to find how often the quality I discerned came from just such a sorrow as my own. It did not comfort me, for I could not rejoice in the knowledge that others had the same burden that I had, but it made me realize that others had learned how to live with it, and so could I. I suppose that was the beginning of the turn. For the despair into which I had sunk when I realized that nothing could be done for the child and that she would live on and on had become a morass into which I could easily have sunk into uselessness. Despair so profound and absorbing poisons the whole system and destroys thought and energy.

My own natural health, too, I suppose, had something
to do with it. I saw that the sun rose and set, that the seasons
came and went, that my garden bloomed and that upon the
streets the people passed and laughter could be heard.

At any rate, the process of accommodation began. The
first step was acceptance of what was. Perhaps it was
consciously taken in a day. Perhaps there was a single
moment in which I actually said to myself. "This thing is
unchangeable, it will not leave me, no one can help me, I
must accept it." But practically the step had to be taken
many times. I slipped into the morass over and over again.
The sight of a neighbor's normal little daughter talking and
doing the things my child could never do was enough to
send me down. But I learned not to stay down. I came up
again and learned to say, "This is my life and I have to live
it."

Having to live a life, it seemed rational as time went on
to try to enjoy what I could in that life. Music was still too
close to me, but there were other things I could enjoy—
books, I remember, were first. Flowers, I think, came next.
I began to care, mildly, about my roses. It all began, I
remember, in a sort of wonder that such things went on as
they had before, and then a realization that what had
happened to me had changed nothing except myself.

Yet life did not really begin again until necessity drove
me to think what I ought to do about the child's life. There
were certain practical things that could and should be done.
Was I to keep her with me, or should she find a home among
children of her own kind? Would she be happier with me
or with them? Had there been security in her life with me,

I would have felt it best to keep her with me, for I did not believe that anyone could understand her as well as I did, or do for her what I could. Moreover, I had given her birth and she was my responsibility.

It was then that the solitary place in which she stood became apparent to me. The world is not shaped for the helpless. If I should die too young, what would become of her? We were living in China. The best that could be expected was that she would be taken to our country, the United States, and put into an institution. There, alone, she would have to make the adjustment of being without me and without her loving Chinese nurse and all that had meant home to her. She might not be able to make such an adjustment alone. Certainly she would not be able to understand why it had to be, and the puzzle and grief might disturb her beyond control. It came to me then that it would be best for her to make the adjustment while I lived, while I could help. She could gradually change her roots from this home in a new one, knowing that I was near and would come to see her again and again.

Upon this matter of her future security alone I made my decision. It was hastened, perhaps, by a situation peculiar to my life: that China was upset by civil wars and revolutions. I think my decision took its final shape on a certain day, of which I have written elsewhere, when a horde of communist soldiers forced Americans and other foreigners out of their homes, killed some of them and compelled the rest of us to hide for our lives. A kindly Chinese gave us the shelter of her little thatched hut, and there through that long day I faced death with all my family. But it was of my child that I thought most. If the moment of death came, I must contrive to have her killed first. I could not leave her in the hands of wild soldiers.

This situation, as I say, was peculiar, and of no moment to those for whom I write this story. But the essential question remains the same for all of us who have these children who never grow up. We have to think beyond our own lives for them.

It became apparent, too, as time went on, that my little daughter should find her own companions. The friends who came and went in my home could never be her friends. Kind and pitying as they were, they felt the child a strain upon them and they in turn were a strain upon her and upon me. It became clear indeed that I must seek and find her world and put her in it.

Again an incident, very slight in itself, crystallized my thinking. We had some American neighbors in our big Chinese community, and one of the neighbors had a little girl just the age of mine. They had gone to each other's parties. One day, however, the other little girl, having come over to play, was prattling as little girls will, and she said, "My mamma says don't have your poor little girl any more to my party, and so I can't ever have her next time."

Next time, indeed, the invitation did not come. The great separation had begun. I realized then that I must find another world for my child, one where she would not be despised and rejected, one where she could find her own level and have friends and affection, understanding and appreciation. I decided that day to find the right institution for her.

I might mention another circumstance peculiar to my situation. When I told one or two of my closest Chinese friends what I had decided upon, they were very much perturbed. Chinese do not believe in institutions. They feel that the helpless, young and old, should be cared for by the family, reasoning, and quite truly, that no stranger, however kind, can be trusted to be as kind as the family. There are no homes for the old in China, no orphanages except those started through western influence, no places for the insane or for the mentally defective. Such persons are cared for entirely at home, as long as they live. My Chinese friends therefore thought me very cruel to consider letting my child leave home. In vain I explained to them that the American family was not like theirs. The Chinese home is stable and it continues in the same house from generation to generation. All generations live under the same roof and are mutually responsible for and to one another. It is true that such a family home is ideal for the care of the helpless.

They could not believe that I had no such home even in my native land. My relatives were strange to me, since I had grown up far from them, and certainly they could not be expected to look after my helpless child were I to die. Moreover, they lived in separate homes of their own. They would consider it an imposition to have my child left in their care. Ours is an individualistic society, indeed, and the state must do for the individual what family does in the older civilizations. It was hard to explain this to my Chinese friends, and hard not be moved by their appeals to me to keep the child with me.

The decision made, the next question was how it was to be done, and then when. I had found out enough to know that the sort of place I wanted my child to live in would cost money that I did not have. There was no one to pay for this except myself. I must myself devise means to do what I wanted to do for my child.

I am speaking now entirely about myself, and I realize that what I did cannot always be done. The fact is I had never considered money from the days when I first began to earn my own living, at least in part, when I was seventeen years old and in college. Independence had taught me that the important thing was to know what I wanted. Then I could always find means to get it. This habit of mine held. I decided that when the time came I would return to my country and search for the place which could become my child's home.

There is infinite relief in a decision. It provides a goal. A guiding rope was flung into the morass and I clung to it and dragged myself out of despair day by day, as the goal became more clear to me. Knowing what I was going to do and thinking how to do it did not heal the inescapable sorrow, but it helped me to live with it. I ceased to use all my spiritual energies in rebellion. I did not ask *why* so continually. The real secret of it was that I began to stop thinking of myself and my sorrow and began to think only of my child. This meant that I was not struggling against life, but slowly and sometimes blindly coming into accord with it. So long as I centered in myself, life was unbearable. When I shifted that center even a little, I began to understand that sorrow could be borne, not easily but possibly.

I felt, however, that before I let my child leave me I ought to try her abilities for myself and learn to know her thoroughly, so that I could make the best possible choice of her future home. For this I decided to take a year, during which all my time, aside from family essentials, would be spent with her. I would try to teach her to read, to write, to distinguish colors and, since she loved music, to learn notes and to sing little songs. Whether she could do this I did not know. It was as important for me to know if she could not as to know if she could.

In a curious way I was helped here by what was taking place in China. The rowdy capture of Nanking by the new revolutionary forces had compelled all white people to leave the city for a period. It was in early spring that the capture took place, and we went to Japan for a peaceful summer in the beautiful green mountains above the seaport of Nagasaki. It was a happy summer in its way. We lived in a small Japanese house in the woods, and bereft of posses-sions and responsibilities, it was a return to nature. For me, after the hard years, it was a time of healing. I knew no one except the friendly Japanese fisherfolk who came to sell crabs and fish at early morning. My child could run about as she liked, while I did my primitive housekeeping. I cooked on a charcoal brazier as the Japanese women did, and we lived upon rice and fish and fruit.

I shall pause here for a little gift of thanks to the Japanese people I met in those pleasant months of enforced holiday. Later in the summer I decided to take advantage of idleness and to make a journey through Japan. With my child I made that journey, traveling third class by day on the trains, both to save money and to meet the average Japanese people. We ate the little lunches we bought from vendors at the station, small clean wooden boxes packed with compartments of rice, pickles and fish, and my child for the first time in her life had fresh pasteurized milk, hot and in sealed bottles.

At night we left the train and slept in clean little village inns where we saw only Japanese faces. We left our shoes at the doorway, and deft Japanese maids put slippers on our feet and led us to a hot bath and then to our room. Then the evening meal was served in lacquered wooden bowls, a chicken or beef broth, eggs, fish, rice and tea. Afterward the spotless soft quilts were brought from the wall closets, and spread on the clean matting floor for us. I woke often in the night to gaze into a dim moonlit garden, perhaps only a few feet square, which somehow suggested, nevertheless, space and infinity. It is the Japanese genius. Everywhere we met with kindness and courtesy. There was no sign that anyone saw my child as strange. She was accepted for what she was and most tenderly treated. That brought healing too.

In the late autumn, before Christmas, we went back to China to live for a year in Shanghai. It was still not safe, we were told, to return to Nanking. That year alone with my child was a profound education for me. As I look back on it, I see that it was the beginning of whatever real knowledge I have of the human mind. We had three rooms at the top of a house shared with two other families, refugees like ourselves. There I planned my child's days and my own, so much time each day devoted to finding out what she could learn. I willed myself to patience and submission to her capacities. Impatience was a sin. So the long year began, work interspersed with exercise and play.

The detail of those months is unimportant now, but I will simply say that I found that the child could learn to read simple sentences, that she was able, with much effort, to write her name, and that she loved songs and was able to sing simple ones. What she was able to achieve was of no significance in itself. I think she might have been able to proceed further, but one day, when, pressing her always very gently but still steadily and perhaps in my anxiety rather relentlessly, I happened to take her little right hand to guide it in writing a word. It was wet with perspiration. I took both her hands and opened them and saw they were wet. I realized then that the child was under intense strain, that she was trying her very best for my sake, submitting to something she did not in the least understand, with an angelic wish to please me. She was not really learning anything.

It seemed my heart broke all over again. When I could control myself I got up and put away the books forever. Of what use was it to push this mind beyond where it could function? She might after much effort be able to read a little, but she could never enjoy books. She might learn to write her name, but she would never find in writing a means of communication. Music she could hear with joy, but she could not make it. Yet the child was human. She had a right to happiness, and her happiness was to be able to live where she could function.

"Let's go outside and play with the kittens," I said.

Her little face took on a look of incredulous joy, and that was my reward.

Happiness, I now determined, was to be her atmosphere. I gave up all ambition for her, all pride, and accepted her exactly as she was, expecting nothing, grateful if some flash came through the dimness of her mind. Wherever she could be most happy would be her home. I kept her with me until she was nine years old, and then I set out in search of her final home.

III

I came to my own country as a stranger. There was disadvantage in this, for I had no friends to guide me, nor any who knew in any way what I needed or how to help me. Yet there was advantage too. I knew what I wanted to find and I had learned from my life among the Chinese to look for essentials—that is, for human quality. I had to determine that I would not judge by money alone. If the right place cost a great deal, I would find some way to pay for it. I was young, I was strong, I was well educated. With those three gifts, I could provide somehow for the child.

I learned a great deal in the next year. It took me in many directions indeed. I had a long list of schools and institutions and I asked for others as I went. Of that intensive search it would be useless to tell every detail, but for those who must make a similar search it may be useful to know certain things.

First of all, I learned not to judge an institution by its grounds and equipment. Some of the finest and most expensively equipped schools were the worst, so far as the children were concerned. I remember one such place. I had spent a whole day with the headmistress. She showed me every detail of the splendidly planned grounds and houses. The children were well fed and well cared for, obviously. She had a resident doctor and a resident psychologist. The attendants for the children were neat and pleasant. There were an excellent school building and a good exhibit of handcraft, done by the children. There was a department of music. Every effort, she assured me, was made to develop the children to the height of their potentiality. She herself was competent, brisk, not unkind. I tried to think of my little girl beside her and could not quite imagine warmth between them, but of course the headmistress would not have much to do with any individual child. So well impressed was I as the day went on that I was beginning to think of the fabulous annual fee and to plan how it could be found. Evening came, and I sat on the wide porch, still with the headmistress, waiting for the bus that was to take me away. Then something happened which undid all the day.

A car stopped and a group of young girls in their teens, all children in the school, mounted the steps and crossed the porch. They greeted the headmistress very properly and she returned their greeting. I saw her watching them sharply.

Suddenly she called to them, "Girls, stop!"

They stopped, half frightened.

The headmistress said in her clear, peremptory way, "How often have I told you to hold up your heads? Go back to the steps and walk across the porch again."

They obeyed instantly while she watched.

When they had gone into the house she turned to me with a complacent explanatory air. "It is part of my work to teach the girls how to enter a room properly and how to leave it. Feeble-minded people always walk with their heads hanging—it's characteristic. I have to break them of it."

"Why?" I asked.

She shrugged her shoulders. "These girls all come of good families, people in society," she explained. "The

parents don't want to be ashamed of taking them about."
She laughed half contemptuously. "Why, I even have to
teach them how to hold a hand at bridge and look as though
they were playing!"

"Why do you do it?" I asked.

"I have to make my living," she said honestly enough.

We parted on that, but I knew that I would never send
my child to her handsome institution. I wanted to find a
man or woman who thought of the children first. Of course
we must all live, but it is amazing how easy it is to find
bread when one does not put it first.

That experience taught me thereafter to look for the
right person at the head of the institution. I knew that the
employees would be no better than the head, therefore the
head must be the best. I ceased to look at equipment and
housing. There must of course be space for play, and ample
sunshine and fresh air. I rejected the extreme north country
because the season outside was so short. My child had been
used to a semi-tropical air and much outdoor play. But
beyond space and a minimum of cleanliness and care, I
began to look for the right people, people who were warm
and human.

I might say here that since I was not resident in my own
country I belonged to no state and therefore state institutions were not easily open to me. Moreover, they had long
waiting lists, and though I visited them, most of them were
overcrowded and the children lived in strict routine. Oh,
how my heart suffered for those big rooms of children
sitting dully on benches, waiting!

"What are they waiting for?" I asked my guide one day.

"They aren't waiting for anything," he replied in surprise. "They're just sitting. That's all they want to do."

"How do you know they wouldn't like to do something more?" I asked.

He evaded the question. "We get them all up a couple of times a day and make them walk around the building."

But I know the children were really waiting. They were waiting for something pleasant to happen to them. Perhaps they did not know they were waiting, but they were. I know now that there is no mind so dim that it does not feel pain and pleasure. These, too, were human beings—that, I perceived, was the important thing to understand, and many of those who cared for them did not understand it. The children who never grow are human beings and they suffer as human beings, inarticulately but deeply nevertheless. The human creature is always more than an animal.

That is the one thing we must never forget. He is forever more than a beast. Though the mind has gone away, though he cannot speak or communicate with anyone, the human stuff is there, and he belongs to the human family.

I saw this wonderfully exemplified in one state institution. When I first visited the place it was an abode of horror. The children, some young in body, some old, were apparently without any minds whatever. The average mental age was estimated at less than one year. They were herded together like dogs. They wore baglike garments of rough calico or burlap. Their food was given to them on the floor and they snatched it up. No effort was made to teach them toilet habits. The floors were of cement and were hosed two or three times a day. The beds were pallets on the floor, and filthy. There were explanations, of course. I was told that these children could be taught nothing, that they merely existed until they died. Worst of all to me was that there was not one thing of beauty anywhere, nothing for the children to look at, no reason for them to lift their heads or put out their hands.

Some years later I went back again. I had heard there was a new man in charge, a young man who was different. I found that he was different, and because he was, he had made the whole institution different. It was as crowded as ever, but wholly changed. It was like a home. There were gay curtain at the windows and bright linoleum on the floors. In the various rooms the children had been segregated, babies were with babies, and older children with their own kind. There were chairs and benches and the children sat on them. There were flowers in the windows and toys on the floor. The children were decent and even wore pretty clothes, and they were all clean. The old sickening smell was gone. There was a dining room, and there were tables, on which were dishes and spoons and mugs.

"Are the children now of a higher grade?" I asked the young man.

"No," he said, smiling, "many of them are the same children."

"But I was told they could not be taught."

"They can all be taught something," he replied. "When they can't manage alone, someone helps them."

Then he showed me the things they had made, actually little baskets and mats, simple and full of mistakes, but to me wonderful. And the children who had made them were so proud of what they had done. They came up to us, and though they could not speak, they knew what they had done.

"Has their mental age gone up?" I asked.

"A little, on the average," he replied. "But it isn't only mental age that counts with them—or with anybody, for that matter."

"How did you do it?" I asked.

"I treat them as human beings," he said simply.

When my search ended it was at another place where I found such a person. Without looking at the buildings or the grounds, I knew when I entered the office and shook hands with quiet, gray-haired man who greeted me with a gentle voice that I had found what I wanted. Of course I did not decide upon impulse. I told him about my child and what it was that I looked for, and he listened. There was something in the way he listened. He was sympathetic, but not with effort. He was not eager. He said diffidently that he did not know whether I would be satisfied with his school, but we might look around. So we did look around, and what I saw was that every child's face lit when he came into the cottages, and that there was a clamor of voices to greet him and call his name—Uncle Ed, they called him. I saw he took time to play with them and that he let them hug his knees and look in his pockets where there were small chocolates—very tiny ones, not enough to spoil a child's appetite. He knew every child and his seeing eyes were noticing everything everywhere. He greeted the attendants with courtesy and when he made a suggestion—that

Jimmy, for instance, should have a lower chair upon which to sit, and so the legs of the chair he liked best could be cut off to suit—the attendant was quick to agree.

The buildings were pleasant and adequate, but not nearly so handsome as some I had seen. The atmosphere was what I felt. It was warm and free and friendly. I saw children playing around the yards behind the cottages, making mud pies and behaving as though they were at home. I saw a certain motto repeated again and again on the walls, on the stationery, hanging above the head's own desk. It was this: "Happiness first and all else follows."

The head smiled when he saw my eyes resting on the words. "That's not just sentimentality," he said. "It is the fruit of experience. We've found that we cannot teach a child anything unless his mind and heart are free of unhappiness. The only child who can learn is the happy child."

I knew enough about teaching to know that this is a sound principle in any education. It was comforting and reassuring to find it the cornerstone here upon which all else was built. I said to myself that I would look no more.

Upon a September day I bought my little girl to the place I had found. We walked about to accustom her to the new playgrounds and I went with her to the corner where her bed stood. I met the woman who was to be her attendant, as well as the superintendent of girls. The child clung to my hand and I to hers. What went on in her little mind I do not know, but I think some foreboding was there. We had never been separated, and the time was coming when there must be a separation almost as final as death. I would come back to see her often, and she could come sometimes to see me, but the separation was there, nevertheless. We were to be parted. Even though I believed that it was best for her safety that she find her permanent shelter here, the fact that she would need lifelong shelter was the primary cruelty.

In the afternoon of that day which was so dreadful in its passing the head asked me to come to the assembly hall. The children were all to gather there for some music. In his kindness he asked me to sit on the platform with him and to speak to the children for a few minutes about Chinese children. Some of them, he said, would understand.

There are moments which crystallize within an instant the meaning of years. Such a one came to me when I stood on the platform of that room and saw before me hundreds of children's faces looking up to me. What heartache loomed behind each one, what years of pain, what tears, what frightened disappointment and despair! They were here for life, prisoners of their fate. And among them, one of them, my child must henceforth be.

The kind man at whose side I stood must have discerned something of what I felt, for when he saw I could not speak he told a little story and made the children laugh and I was able to go on again. I think I never tried more earnestly to interest an audience, never had I put myself so wholehear-tedly into any effort as I did that half hour of talk with those children. I could not say what was in my heart. I could not tell them I understood their lives better than I understood anything else, because I had lived through such a life. I had to tell small childish things that they could grasp, and my reward was their fresh laughter.

After it was over, the head took me aside alone and talked to me gently and gravely. I have never forgotten his words. "You must remember," he said, "that these are happy children. They are safe here. They will never know distress or want. They will never know struggle or defeat, nor will sorrow ever touch them. No demands are made upon them which they cannot meet. The joys which they can appreciate they have. Your child will escape all suffering. Will you remember that and let it be a comfort to you? Remember that there is a sorrow worse than one's own—it is to see a beloved person suffer without being able to help. That sorrow you will never have."

Many a time since then when I have thought of the child and the waters have seemed to close over my head, I have remembered those kind and wise words. As long as the child is happy, am I not strong enough to bear what is to be borne?

I left her there and, following the request of the school, I did not visit her for a month. The head believed that a full month was needed for the new roots to be put down, and to see the parents delayed the necessary process. They would tell me, he promised, if anything went wrong. So I tore myself away, leaving her for the first time in our lives.

Of that month I need not speak. Any parent like me will know the doubts that beset me. To leave a child who cannot write a letter, who cannot even make known in words what she feels and needs, seemed to me at times the height of cruelty. These times came in the night, and only the thought of a future with the child grown old and me gone could keep me from hurrying to the nearest railway station. Ah, well, there are many who know such hours in the night!

It would be pleasant to say that when I went back to the school at the end of the month I found the child happy and well. This was not true. Her distraught little face, her pitiful joy at seeing me brought back all the doubts again and I was ready to pack her trunk and bring her home.

The elderly matron stood looking at us. "She has been quite naughty," she said gravely. "She has not wanted to do what the other children do and she has cried a great deal. We have had to deal with her."

"Deal with her?" I asked.

"Yes. When she ran out of the house we had to restrain her."

"She is used to freedom," I murmured. "And of course she was running out to look for me."

"She cannot run outside alone," the matron said, "and she must learn to obey. When she learns, she will be happy as the others are."

Protest was thick in my throat, but I choked it back. "I will take her out for a little walk," I said.

As soon as we were outside and alone she was as happy as a songbird again, but she clutched my hand as though she would never let it go. I went in search of the head. He was there in his office and he welcomed me and spoke to the child. She seemed to know him and not be afraid of him, and this meant he had been to see her himself.

I began at once. "I think I cannot leave her here," I told him. "The matron says that they have had to restrain her, whatever that means. But surely they understand that a little child like this cannot suddenly be happy without the home she has always had. She has never been among strangers. She cannot understand why her life is completely and suddenly changed. Do the children have to be forced into a routine? Must they walk in line into the dining room, for example?"

This and much more I said. He let me say it all while his eyes were kind upon us.

"It is not possible for your child to live here exactly as she has in your home," he said when I had finished. "Here she is one of many. She will be individually cared for and watched and taught, it is true, but she cannot behave as though she were the only child. This will mean some loss of freedom to her. This loss you must weigh against the gain. She is safe here. She has companionship. When she learns to fall in with the others in the small routines that are necessary in any big family, she will even enjoy the sense of being with the crowd. She has to learn, you know. But rest assured that she will be taught only those things which she is able to learn and nothing will be forced on her that is beyond her.

"Try to think of what she will be a year from now, five years from now. Try to consider justly whether this place is the right one for her home. Don't lose a larger value in some small present dissatisfaction."

I said, "It is so hard because she doesn't understand why it is all necessary or that it is for her good."

"None of us really understands why," he said in his same gentle voice. "You do not understand why you have had to have the child like this at all. You cannot see that there is any good in it anywhere."

I could not indeed.

"You cannot shield your child from everything," he went on. "She is a human creature and she must bear her little share, too, of what is common to all human life."

Much else he said and I sat listening and the child sat content by my side. When he finished I knew that he had done what he meant to do—he had helped me to find strength to think of the child's larger good.

I stayed with her for only a day because they said it would be better not to stay too long the first time. Then I went away. I shall never forget as long as I live that I had to pull her little arms away from around my neck and that I dared not look back. I knew the matron was holding her fast and I knew I must not see it, lest my courage fail.

Years have passed since that day. I came to live in America, not far from her, and I visit her often. She is used now to my coming and going, and yet even now there is the brief clinging when I leave. "I want to go home," she whispers again and again. She comes home sometimes, too, and is filled with joy for a few days. But here is the comfort I take nowadays. After she has been at home a week or so, she begins to miss the other home. She inquires after "the girls," she asks for some toy or musical instrument or record that she left behind. At last almost willingly she goes back again, after making sure that I am coming soon to see her. The long struggle is over. The adjustment has been made. When the wakeful hours come in the night I comfort myself, thinking that if I should die before I wake, as the old childish prayer has it, her life would go on just the same. Much of the money that I have been able to earn has gone into making this security for her. I have a sense of pride that she will be dependent on no one as long as she lives, and whether or not I live I have done all that could be done.

I realize that many parents cannot be so fortunate as I have been in being able to make a child secure. Some of them have come to me with children like mine and have asked me what to do. They have told me that they have little money or that they have other children and what there is must be divided. The helpless child cannot have everything, however the parents' hearts are torn. They are right, of course. Speaking coldly, if it is possible to do so, the normal children are more useful to society perhaps than the helpless ones.

And yet I wonder if that is so. My helpless child has taught me so much. She has taught me patience, above all else. I come of a family impatient with stupidity and slowness, and I absorbed the family intolerance of minds less quick than our own. Then there was put into my sole keeping this pitiful mind, struggling against I know not what handicap. Could I despise it for what was no fault of its own? That indeed would have been the most cruel injustice. While I tried to find out its slight abilities I was compelled both by love and justice to learn tender and careful patience. It was not always easy. Normal impatience burst forth time and again, to my shame, and it seemed useless to try to teach. But justice reasoned with me thus: "This mind has the right to its fullest development too. It may be very little, but the right is the same as yours, or any other's. If you refuse it the right to know, in so far as it can know, you do a wrong."

So by this most sorrowful way I was compelled to tread, I learned respect and reverence for every human mind. It was my child who taught me to understand so clearly that all people are equal in their humanity and that all have the same human rights. None is to be considered less, as a human being, than any other, and each must be given his place and his safety in the world. I might never have learned this in any other way. I might have gone on in the arrogance of my own intolerance for those less able than myself. My child taught me humanity.

My child taught me to know, too, that mind is not all of the human creature. Though she cannot speak to me clearly, there are other ways in which she communicates. She has an extraordinary integrity of character. She seems to sense deception and she will not tolerate it. She is a child of great purity. She will not tolerate habits that are filthy and her sense of dignity is complete. No one may take liberties with her person. Neither will she endure cruelty. If a child in her cottage screams she hurries to see why, and if the child is being struck by another child or if an attendant is too harsh, she cries aloud and goes in search of the housemother. She has been known to push away the offending one. She will not endure injustice. An attendant, laughing, said to me one day, "We have to treat her fairly or she makes more trouble for us."

What I am trying to say is that there is a whole personality not concerned with the mind, and children mentally deficient often compensate for their lack by other qualities of goodness.

This is a very important fact and it has been so recognized. Psychologists working with mentally retarded children at The Training School in Vineland, New Jersey, have found that while I.Q. may be very low indeed a child actually may function a good deal higher because of his social sense, his feeling of how he ought to behave, his pride, his kindness, his wish to be liked. Acting upon this observation, they developed the Social Maturity Scale, to complement the Binet Scale earlier brought from France and adapted for use in the United States. What is true of the retarded child is also true of the normal one. A high intelligence may be a curse to society, as it has often been, useless it is accompanied by qualities of character which provide social maturity, and the less brilliant child who has these qualities is a better citizen and often achieves more individually than the high intelligence without them.

Today this Vineland Social Maturity Scale is very widely used in the armed forces, in schools and colleges, in aptitude tests, wherever normal individuals are measured. We have to thank the helpless children for teaching us that mere intelligence is not enough.

They have taught us much more. They have taught us how people learn. The minds of retarded children are sane minds, normal except that, being arrested, the processes are slowed. But they learn in the same ways that the normal minds do, repeated many more times. Psychologists, observing the slower processes, have been able to discover, exactly as though in a slow-motion picture, the way the human creature acquires new knowledge and new habits. Our educational techniques for normal children have been vastly improved by what the retarded children have taught us.

In the years which have passed since I led my child into her own world, again and again I have been able to find comfort in the fact that her life, with others, has been of use in enlarging the whole body of our knowledge. When one has learned how to live with inescapable sorrow, one learns, too, how to find comfort by the way.

When I speak of comfort I think now of other parents than myself. I think of those who bring me their children and ask what to do for them. Almost the first question they ask is, "Are private schools and institutions so much better than the state ones that we ought to make all the family sacrifice to the utmost for the sake of one?"

My answer is this: A good private school is usually better than the average state institution. There is less crowding and more individual attention. But even this depends somewhat upon the state. There are states where the institutions are remarkably good, the employees well paid, a pension system established and every inducement offered for good people to say. There are other states where the institutions are medieval. Parents must examine their own state institutions. Where there are ample family funds, a good private institution has advantages. Yet the weakness in most institutions is that often they do not continue beyond the lifetime of the person who establishes them. Some of the finest and most elaborate private institutions will close when the head dies, and the children then must be scattered and must make their adjustments all over again. It is essential in choosing your child's home that you find an institution which is not dependent upon any one man, but which is controlled by a self-perpetuating board of trustees and has endowments to carry it through the hard years. The state institutions have, of course, an immense advantage in that they are permanent, and once a child enters he is secure for life.

I answer the parents by saying that where a private institution would bring severe sacrifice on every member of the family for the sake of one, I would find a good state institution, even if I had to move my home to another state, and there I would put my child.

When the child is safely in his new home, what are the further responsibilities of the parent? They are many. The child needs the parents as much as before. There should be regular visits, as frequent as possible. Do not think that the children do not know. I have to endure heartbreaking moments every time I go to visit my child, for inevitably some other little child comes and takes my hand and leans against me and asks, "Where is my mamma?"

The housemother whispers over her head, "Poor little thing, her folks never come to see her. Her grandmother came to see her two years ago and that's the last."

The little thing's heart is slowly breaking. For these children are always children. They are loving and affectionate and they crave to be loved exactly as all children do. There are other children who come to tell me, eyes glowing, "My daddy and mommy came last week to see me!" Even the ones who cannot speak will come to show me a new doll that the parents brought.

Ah, they know, because they feel! The mind seems to have very little to do with the capacity to feel.

Another responsibility of the parent is to watch always the person in direct charge of the child. I said that I chose my child's permanent home by finding as the head the sort of person whom I could trust. Today, were I to choose again, I would also go into every cottage and look at the type of attendant there. Were they the hard-faced professional type, the ones who go from institution to institution, callous, cruel, ready to strike a child who does not conform, I would reject that place. For the most important person in an institution, so far as the child is concerned, and therefore so far as the parent is concerned, is not the executive, and not the man or woman in the offices, not even the doctor and the psychologist and the teacher, but the attendant, the person who has the direct care of the child.

A cruel and selfish attendant who has not at heart the welfare of the child can undo all the work of the teacher and the psychologist. Your child cannot benefit by any teaching unless he is happy in his daily life in his cottage. The attendant must be a person of affectionate and invincibly kind nature, child loving, able to discipline without physical force, in control because the children love him or her. Whether this attendant is well educated is not important. He must understand children, for he has in his care perpetual children.

Any sign of cruelty or injustice or carelessness on the part of attendants should be at once reported by conscientious parents. Do not think that secret bribes or tips will protect your child from a bad attendant. He will take your money and when he is alone with the children, as he is so much of the time, he will treat your child exactly as he does the others.

A third responsibility which the parent has to the child in the institution is to see that the atmosphere in which he lives is one of hopefulness. I have observed that this atmosphere is best in those institutions which carry on research as one of their functions. A place where the care is merely custodial is apt to degenerate into something routine and dead. No child ought to be merely something to be cared for and preserved from harm. His life, however simple, means something. He has something to contribute, even though he is helpless. There are reasons for his condition, causes which may be discovered. If he himself cannot be cured or even changed, others may be born whole because of what he has been able to teach, all unknowingly.

The Training School at Vineland is an excellent example of what I mean. For many years it has maintained an active research department. As I said, it was the first institution in this country to use and adapt the Binet test, and there the Social Maturity Scale was developed. Its work with birth-injured children and cerebral palsy has been notable, and the vigorous men and woman who have spent their lives there learning from the children, in order that they may know better how to prevent and to cure, have infused vitality into the life of the institution, and into the whole subject of mental deficiency beyond.

Parents may find comfort, I say, in knowing that their children are not useless, but that their lives, limited as they are, are of great potential value to the human race. We learn as much from sorrow as from joy, as much from illness as from health, from handicap as from advantage—and indeed perhaps more. Not out of fullness has the human soul always reached its highest, but often out of deprivation. This is not to say that sorrow is better than happiness, illness than health, poverty than richness. Had I been given the choice, I would a thousand times over have chosen to have my child sound and whole, a normal woman today, living a woman's life. I miss eternally the person she cannot be. I am not resigned and never will be. Resignation is something still and dead, an inactive acceptance that bears no fruit. On the contrary, I rebel against the unknown fate that fell upon her somewhere and stopped her growth. Such things ought not to be, and because it has happened to me and because I know what this sorrow is I devote myself and my child to the work of doing all we can to prevent such suffering for others.

There is one little boy in my child's school whom I often go to see. He is little because he is only about seven in his mind. His body now is almost forty years old. He has a grave face and there is a forlorn look in his eyes. His father is a famous man, wealthy and well known. But he never comes to see his son. The boy's mother is dead. When someone approached this father for a gift for a new kind of research he banged his desk with his fist and said, "I will not give one cent! All my money is going to normal people."

Callous? He is not callous. His heart is bleeding, his pride is broken. His son is an imbecile—*his* son! In these years he has thought of himself and his loss, and he has missed the joy he might have had in his child—not the joy he sought, of course, but joy for all that.

There is another father—they are not always fathers, either—whose boy loves to work with the cows. I see the lad sometimes, a handsome fellow. He is usually in the dairy barn, caring for the cows, brushing them clean, loving them. I saw his father there one day, that brilliant able man, and he said, "It does seem that if my boy can learn to use the milking machine he could learn to do something better."

The head happened to be there that day and he said, "But there is nothing better for him, don't you see? The best thing in the world for each of us is that which we can best do, because it gives us the feeling of being useful. That's happiness."

So what I would say to parents is something I have learned through the years and it took me long to learn it, and I am still learning. When your little child is born to you not whole and sound as you had hoped, but warped and defective in body or mind or perhaps both, remember this is still your child. Remember, too, that the child has his right to life, whatever that life may be, and he has the right to happiness, which you must find for him. Be proud of your child, accept him as he is and do not heed the words and stares of those who know no better. This child has a meaning for you and for all children. You will find a joy you cannot now suspect in fulfilling his life for and with him. Lift up your head and go your appointed way.

I speak as one who knows.

Yet none of us lives in the past, if we are still alive ourselves. It is inevitable that, as young parents in their time experience again the old agony and despair when their children are among those who can never grow, they demand some cause for hope. Other ills have been cured and research is being carried on for those we still do not know how to heal. All must be healed, of course. People must not die of cancer or polio or heart disease. Neither should they be mentally deficient if it can be prevented or cured. There cannot be a choice of which will be first. The battle of life must be fought on all fronts at the same time.

Therefore, I say, we must also fight for the right of our children to be born sound and whole. There must not be children who cannot grow. Year by year their number must be decreased until preventable causes of mental deficiency are prevented. The need is more pressing than the public knows. Our state institutions are dangerously overcrowded and unless research is hastened, millions of dollars must go into more institutions. Even if boarding homes are multiplied, care of these children must be paid for, in the vast majority of cases, by public funds. How much wiser and more hopeful it would be to pay for scientific research which would make such care unnecessary! Let us remember that more than half of the mentally deficient in this country are so from noninherited causes, and these causes can be prevented, did we know what they are.*

Present care, moreover, is very inadequate. State institutions are able to provide very little of the education that might release a good many of the children to normal, if protected, life. It is not possible to do much educating with an overworked staff in an overcrowded institution. In some states the higher positions in these institutions are still political plums, and the lives of the children are at the mercy of a succession of ignorant men. Private institutions, if they are good ones, are too expensive for the average family.

Yet I believe that the private institution has an indispensable place in our American system. Our notable scientific advance has been the result of private persons working in privately owned places. Public funds have developed very little scientific knowledge except for military purposes. So now I believe that research into this most necessary field, the study of the causes and cure of mental deficiency, must,

---

* [At present, the number of cases of mental retardation caused by inherited factors is not known. According to The ARC, over 350 causes have been identified, but in 75 percent of the cases, the cause of a child's mental retardation is not known. It is undeniable, however, that the leading cause of mental retardation today—maternal abuse of alcohol or drugs—is preventable.]

in accordance with American tradition, take place in small private institutions where scientists can work in freedom. Such research should be co-ordinated so there will be no time wasted in duplication.

Something, of course, has already been done. I have spoken of the notable work of the Research Department at The Training School in Vineland, New Jersey. We know that at least 50 per cent of the mentally deficient children now in the United States can be educated to be productive members of society. *Education* alone would relieve our overcrowded public institutions. Studies have shown that there are nineteen types of jobs that can be done by an adult whose mentality is no more than that of a six-year-old child. Twenty per cent of all work in the United States is done by the unskilled worker.

We know, too, some of the reasons for injury to the brain, both prenatal and postnatal, but we do not know enough. A little physical remedial work is being done for the injured brains which are the chief causes of mental deficiency, but it is still experimental and confined largely to the limited though important field of cerebral palsy, where the decreased blood supply to the brain is the apparent cause for mental deficiency.* Results are still too new to be relied upon, but in one institution they were reported as hopeful: 34 per cent of those operated upon

---

*   [Today it is known that cerebral palsy can be caused by many types of injuries to the brain before birth, during birth, or shortly after birth. Decreased blood supply is only one possible cause of brain injury.]

showed definite mental improvement, an additional 51 per cent showed changes for the better in alertness, muscular control, interest span, appetite and increased irritability.

I speak of all this merely as grounds for hope, if and when research really begins in the causes and cure for mental deficiency on a scale comparable to that now being done in other fields. Hope is essential for activity.

Those who have children who can never grow—and few are the families who have not one somewhere—must and will work with renewed effort when they realize that more than half the children now mentally deficient need not have been so. They must and will work still harder when they realize that more than half now mentally deficient can, with proper education and environment, live and work in normal society, instead of being idle in inadequate institutions.

Hope brings comfort. What has been need not forever continue to be so. It is too late for some of our children, but if their plight can make people realize how unnecessary much of the tragedy is, their lives, thwarted as they are, will not have been meaningless.

Again, I speak as one who knows.

Afterword
Janice C. Walsh*

I remember the day, in the summer of 1972, when my mother made her last visit to see Carol. She had asked me to drive her down to the school, and my younger sister, Jean, also accompanied us. My mother wanted Carol to get reacquainted with both of us, as she knew that she might not be able to visit again. She was beginning to feel the effects of the lung cancer that was shortly to be diagnosed.

We had arrived at Carol's cottage, a two-story, yellow-brick building which my mother had endowed to the school many years ago. We were in Carol's suite, which included a large, light and airy bedroom furnished with a painted French Provincial bedroom set from the 1930s, as well as a small bath, and a playroom with windows on three sides. Mother was seated in a high-backed chair, and Jean on the window seat, while I stood nearby. My mother spoke to Carol slowly and simply, trying to explain who these other visitors were. At first, Carol seemed somewhat perplexed, but then she turned toward me, and in her own authoritative way told me to sit, as Mother repeated my name several times. I watched Carol's face intently, and saw her expres-

---

* Janice C. Walsh was Carol Buck's sister and legal guardian. She is President of the Board of Directors of the Pearl S. Buck Foundation and has served on the Board of Directors of the Training School at Vineland, New Jersey. She works as an occupational therapist with the mentally retarded.

sion change from confusion to recognition as Mother spoke
the word "Janice." I knew then that the responsibility had
been passed on from mother to daughter. I looked at my
mother's face, and saw the quiet relief and serenity that she
had sought in this visit. It was now my time to accept the
responsibility; to ensure that Carol would continue to have
a family of her own. I would be her link to the past, and to
the present.

Some of our shared past is recounted in *The Child Who
Never Grew*. Many years have passed since the book was
first published, however, and new chapters have been
added to Carol's life. Mother also left a few unanswered
questions in the original story, which can now, I think, be
safely answered. This, then, is Carol's and my story, but
mainly Carol's, drawn from *my* memories of how she grew.

Carol was just five when I was adopted by our parents,
Pearl and Lossing Buck. I was a scrawny three-month-old
child who had not grown, nor gained much weight since I
was born. In fact, I was not expected to survive much past
those months. The mother who adopted me wanted a child
who would fulfill the expectations her own birth child had
been unable to satisfy, and though she had obstacles to
surmount, she was determined to achieve her dream.

Carol and I were happy as we grew up in China. We
played together, and enjoyed our lives together as we
explored the sounds and sights of nature: the sun, the wind,
and the earth. But Carol did not grow as a child should
grow, and I am sure that I sped past her. I don't, however,

Carol and her younger sister,
Janice, photographed in late 1925

have any recollections that my sister and I were developing at a different pace.

Although *The Child Who Never Grew* makes no mention of my father's feelings about Carol, I know that both Pearl and Lossing were concerned about her slow development and her inability to learn past a certain level. Both searched for answers to the enigma that was my sister. Being a very strong-willed person who was unable to admit defeat or accept this reality, my mother searched continuously for explanations, looking for a miracle to make her child well. Lossing, on the other hand, could immerse himself in his work. He had come to Nanking in 1916, determined to teach and to introduce American methods of agriculture, especially in the wheat-growing region of China. Since then he had become acting dean and instructor in Agricultural Economics, Farm Management, Rural Sociology, and Farm Engineering at the university in

Nanking. Lossing had a long and distinguished career and became well-known in China for his work.

Another reason that Lossing was not included in my mother's account is that their paths were slowly going in separate directions during this time. Pearl was beginning to develop her potential as a writer, as she needed to find an outlet for her own deep-rooted insecurity. The parting did not become a reality for several more years after Carol left home, but their break-up was a narrative thread that my mother obviously did not want to weave into the story.

During the years after my parents' divorce, there was little, if any, communication between the two, and I was forbidden to have any relationship with Lossing from the moment my mother and I left China. Lossing remained in China and eventually remarried. He and his Chinese wife had two very bright children who never displayed any genetic problems. It was not until we were reunited after my mother's death in 1973 that I learned how much he had missed me and my sister. He gave me some early photographs of Carol and me that he had kept all these years, even though my mother had asked him to return all his family photos after the divorce. Lossing died in November, 1975, but not before we had had a chance to renew our family ties.

I do not remember that day in 1929 when Carol was taken from me. I was only four, and she was nine, when she was placed in an institution—the Training School at Vineland, New Jersey. Although I realize now that it was for the best, Carol's departure broke up a family within which we each felt comfortable. Carol and I were as close as sisters should be, even though I was too young to recognize or express my feelings.

The years passed slowly, as I continued in my path from boarding school to boarding school. Because I spent so much time away from home, I did not have the opportunity to visit with my sister as I would have wished. But then again, I did not see much of my parents or other siblings, either. My siblings were eleven and twelve years younger than I was, and we had few interests in common.

For many years, my main contact with Carol occurred in the summer, when she would come home to Pennsylvania for visits of a week or so. The housemother from the Training School always came along to supervise her care, as nobody was ever sure how well Carol would adapt to our family, or our family to her. All in all, I think we adapted fairly well. Carol seemed to recognize us during her visits, and we included her in activities such as playing in the wading pool. But we knew that she had her own life, and it was no longer a part of ours. Usually she kept to herself and her own activities.

When I entered Antioch College in Ohio, I, too, found my own life. There I learned about Occupational Therapy, a new field that combined two interests of mine—medicine and the creative use of the mind through the workings of one's own hands. After several years of learning and internship, I became an Occupational Therapist, and have worked in this field since early 1949. For many years, I worked with psychiatric patients, then in Geriatrics, and now, for the past seven years, with the mentally retarded.

About a year after I had launched my career, the first edition of *The Child Who Never Grew* was released. Strange as it may seem, I have no recollection of its publication. One reason may be that I was no longer living at home and was therefore not aware of the flood of letters and visits from parents that the book unleashed. Another reason is that Mother was a prolific writer. I do not remember her ever really discussing *any* of her books with me, except during the time she used the pseudonym "John Sedges" to write about topics other than China. So, although it may have been a painful struggle for my mother to decide to reveal the truth about Carol, the decision obviously did not harm me in any way.

On one of my brief visits home, sometime in the 1960s, Mother told me that she had learned the reason for Carol's mental retardation. Carol had an unusual disease called PKU (phenylketonuria). This condition resulted from an inability to metabolize phenylalanine, an essential amino acid. In addition to causing mental retardation, PKU was also associated with blond hair, blue eyes, eczema of the skin, and an overpowering, musty odor, which was perhaps due to the inability to absorb or process protein. (Carol had all of these attributes.) Mother explained that the condition was inherited, and must have been present in both her genes and Lossing's genes. When we learned about PKU, a method of diagnosing the condition by testing urine samples from the diaper had recently been developed. Today a simple blood test is used to detect the condition in newborns, and a diet low in phenylalanine can prevent mental retardation from developing.

I think my mother had mixed feelings about discovering the cause of Carol's mental retardation. Mostly I remember her relief at learning that she was not completely to blame. But I also feel that she had trouble accepting that her family's genes may have contributed to this disorder. Both her brother, Edgar, and her sister, Grace, also had children with handicaps. (One had a child with severe cerebral palsy, and the other, a child who stuttered abnormally.)

Although the test and treatment for PKU were developed too late to prevent Carol's mental retardation, the title of my mother's book was somewhat misleading. Despite her PKU, Carol *did* grow, both physically and mentally. Over the years, I watched her achieve her own potential, thanks to the loving care and concern of the dedicated staff of the Training School at Vineland. They helped her each step of the way, taking to heart their responsibility to ensure the success of those whose lives and growth were entrusted to them.

For most of her life, Carol went to school during the day. She enjoyed school and the activities that were included in her daily routine, and her structured life was good for her. Although I am sure it was not easy to teach her (her attention span was short and she could be strong-minded), she mastered a variety of academic and functional skills over the years. She never learned to read or write, but she did learn to color, write her name, and verbalize her needs. She also learned to sew simple projects and to master many self-care skills that enhanced her independence. She learned to bathe and dress herself with some supervision, to tie her shoelaces, to be independent in toileting and tooth brushing, and to comb and brush her hair with verbal reminders. She also became skilled at using a fork and spoon after she gave up chopsticks, which she preferred for about the first ten years she was at school.

Outside of the classroom, Carol pursued two main interests: music and sports. The love for music described in *The Child Who Never Grew* continued to deepen until it became, perhaps, Carol's most calming support. In the playroom in her suite, there was an upright piano on which Mother would play nursery songs while they both sang along. Carol also learned to operate her phonograph and play whatever struck her fancy—whether it be children's songs, modern music, or classical symphonic music. She actually preferred children's songs or nursery rhymes and often sang or hummed along with the music. When she did not like a song or a rendition of a song, she would change the record and put it underneath the pile. After records started becoming obsolete, I made sure that Carol always had a radio she could listen to. She enjoyed carrying one around with her, but dropped it often, especially when she forgot to unplug it from the wall. I replaced her radio about twice a year.

Carol also demonstrated a remarkable aptitude for different sports, perhaps because her physical abilities were always far above the norm for individuals with PKU. At an early age, she learned to roller skate proficiently. She always loved her three-wheeled bicycle and rode it around the grounds until the final few years of her life. Throughout the years, she excelled in the Special Olympics, mainly in

Carol Buck at 70

running events, and proved herself proficient in shooting baskets just a few years ago.

As Carol grew older, she was trained to do simple vocational tasks. Probably sometime in her fifties, she was placed in a workshop on the school grounds. Unfortunately, this endeavor did not last long. First, Carol's short attention span made it difficult for her to remain focused on her work. Second, although her fine motor skills were good, she quickly became frustrated when pieces did not fit together easily. And third, there was less one-on-one training than Carol had been accustomed to receiving in school, and she had trouble functioning without this intensive guidance. Finally, the staff at Vineland decided that it was not in Carol's best interest to continue with the vocational training, so another avenue was opened up for her.

Carol became an active participant in the Senior Enrichment Program at the school. She joined a group of adults her age, and began participating in group activities suited to her age and skills. The group members went on field trips, cooked, worked on craft projects, and participated in a variety of other activities you could find in any community-based Senior Center. All activities were supervised by staff members, who continued to help Carol and the others improve their skills.

Besides growing mentally and physically, Carol also developed her own personality. Although sometimes she appeared aloof, she was always a friendly, outgoing person. At times, she could express deep caring—for example, by putting her hand on my shoulder, looking intently into my face, and calling me "Honey." She could be very demanding in a loud, authoritative way, but usually her behavior improved if she was corrected with gentle, persistent firmness. Generally, she got along better with the staff at Vineland than she did with her peers. After all, the staff members were the ones who always assisted her and gave her support and guidance, and to whom she communicated her needs and wants. In the early years, she was close with the housemother who lived in her cottage and oversaw the care of all the girls in the cottage. Later, of course, there were other housemothers. After Vineland stopped using housemothers, there were still many caring women who came in for different shifts during the day and night. Despite Carol's occasional bossiness, she was well liked by the staff. The staff members treated her with jovial good humor, and, frankly, sometimes spoiled her.

After I became Carol's guardian in 1973, I began making quarterly visits to Vineland. For nearly twenty years, we spent many happy times together, enjoying the activities that my sister quietly dictated. Whenever I went to visit, I usually brought her a package of gifts such as clothing, records, a harmonica or similar musical toy, candy, peanuts, and instant coffee and pumpkin pie for our treat. Carol would examine her gifts, and then usually ask to go for a short ride in my car. Then it was back to the senior cottage where she lived. There we ate our treat and listened to the new records. Our visits usually lasted for several hours—Carol always watched me carefully to make sure I did not leave too soon. Carol's speech was not clear, and since I did not see her daily, I often found it difficult to understand her sentences. But when she spoke in clear, single words, I could usually understand what she was trying to express. She seemed to understand me quite well, but I had to keep the communication simple.

Throughout the years since our mother's death, I remained my sister's link to her past, as well as her support in the present. As her only immediate family, I tried to help her feel that she was still a part of someone else's life, even though Mother no longer came to visit. I never tried to explain about Mother's death, partly because Carol never asked about her, and partly because I doubted that she would understand the concept of death. But it was clear that she remembered her family. During one of my early visits, I came across three professional photographs and asked her who they were. To each one, and appropriately, she answered: "Father, Mother, Janice." (My picture had been taken when I was four, and I could see no resemblance to the way I look now.) We each went our own ways, and we each understood the other's independence, but our moments together remained special for us both.

I truly believe that Carol had a good life at Vineland and was able to mature in her own way, despite the lack of close family ties. In March 1992, she celebrated her seventy-second birthday. This was something we had not been certain would occur. In mid-1991 she became ill, and a routine chest x-ray revealed cancer in the left lung. A biopsy confirmed the cancer, and after further testing the decision was made to excise the tumor. Unfortunately, the tests had not shown the extent of the metastasis, so although the operation was performed, the tumor was not removed.

Carol was a good patient, and recovered well from her operations. Mild doses of chemotherapy gave her relief from serious symptoms and she made considerable improvement for the first few months. Then, another chest x-ray disclosed that the cancer was beginning to progress. Carol had no respiratory distress, however, so she was allowed to continue with her daily, active routine. She was carefully monitored, and received the best of care from an attentive and loving staff.

Carol Buck died peacefully in her sleep during the afternoon of September 30, 1992. She had begun to slow down considerably during the preceding weeks, but did not show any discomfort or pain. A simple memorial service was conducted by the staff and residents of the Training School, and interment was on the grounds where she had spent so many years of her life. I know she will be remembered fondly.

If I played a role in shaping Carol's life, I think it is fair to say that she also played a role in shaping *my* life. I think that I became the person I am at least in part because she was my sister. I am not a person who easily judges people by what they can or cannot do, nor do I judge them by what they think, or how they may perform a task. Each of us has a way of doing what we can, and in what manner we can. I have always felt close to those who did not have the abilities to succeed or perform as so-called "normal" people did, but it was not until now, when asked to write this Afterword, that I realized that each of us, no matter what our talents, has our own voice and can help others in our own way.

Another gift that Carol gave me is a special insight into our mother's thoughts and actions. Specifically, I think I understand something about her relationship with her own children, as well as her need to reach out to other children throughout the world. This insight has come only recently, as I have learned more about Carol's early years and my mother's anguish over this birth child. As I look back, I wonder how different her life might have been if it were not for this child. Were the compulsive drives to achieve her monumental goals spurred on by her need for perfection— her need to overcome her feelings of inadequacy caused by the birth of Carol—and her need to provide for the care of this daughter?

During Carol's early years, I do not believe that Pearl's own life was fulfilling. Deep in her heart, I think she felt that she had other needs to attend to. Her own destiny had been set aside while she pursued a life that was common and normal during the 1920s: marriage, children, family. Carol's birth changed all this, and eventually changed my mother's life, as she was driven to find a way to provide for her daughter.

The Child Who Never Grew touches briefly on my mother's quest to find an avenue to provide for the care her child would require. What resources did she have as a teacher, and as the wife of a missionary? The only thing that she knew might help in this dilemma was her desire and ability to write—and what was she to write of but the people closest to her, whose struggles she felt nearest to? And so began the outpouring of her heart to relate the stories of those she saw struggling for life and the fulfillment of their dreams. Slowly but steadily, these stories came to life: *East Wind-West Wind, The Good Earth, The Exile, The Mother, The Fighting Angel, Sons, A House Divided.* . . .

What *The Child Who Never Grew* does *not* delve into was how successful her writing was and how this success sometimes prevented her from nurturing the very family she had sought to provide for. But the fact is, she was quickly recognized for her writings, and was honored by both the Pulitzer and Nobel Prizes within a few short years. She had exploded upon the conscience of the peoples of the world, and she would not relent in her pursuit to examine the many social issues that gripped her attention. Her life at last had meaning.

With her writing a critical and commercial success, Pearl was not only able to provide for the financial needs of her child and herself, but also for members of her new family. At Vineland, she donated funds for the construction of Carol's cottage, which housed about sixteen residents. Besides the suite that Carol occupied, the cottage included bedrooms and baths for the other residents, a large dayroom, a large dining room, a good-sized kitchen for meal preparation, and quarters for the housemother. Pearl also established a lifetime living contract for Carol to remain at the school. Naturally, she continued to provide Carol with clothing, toys, phonographs, roller skates, and anything else that my sister wanted or needed. And she assigned the royalties from the first edition of this book to the Training School, probably as a fund-raising gift.

For her second husband and new family—which eventually grew to include six adopted children in addition to myself—Pearl became the main breadwinner. She re-built an old farm house and acquired additional land, and also paid the salaries of numerous household staff. All the while she maintained a busy schedule of writing, social activities in and outside the home, speaking engagements for causes she supported, and many other activities.

Unfortunately, as she was reaching out to so many, there were times that my mother could not be there for her own family. Although she provided for our material needs, she often did not have the time to take care of our emotional needs. She needed to schedule her time carefully so that she had undisturbed hours to write and answer correspondence. And even when she had time to spend with us, I often felt that she lived in another world from ours, and did not really understand simple, everyday family life. She did not seem attuned to the enjoyment my siblings and I took in ordinary pleasures such as sports, and never seemed to recognize our achievements in this area. She placed intellectual pursuits above all else, and since none of us were particularly intellectual, I guess we were disappointments to her in a way.

My mother did her best to balance the different parts of her life, but as we all know, each of our lives can only reach so far. Only when she was close to death did I finally realize that—although she had reached out to all mankind—she had not been able to attend to some of the smaller details that would have made her life more fulfilling. My mother seemed to be at peace with herself when she died, but I know that she left with many dreams unmet. One of the biggest dreams, I am sure, was to make amends to her children, who did not understand the complexities of her life or the role that she felt she could have played in the world.

This magnificent woman—my mother—left a legacy that could not be duplicated, but she also left lives that would need healing. It cannot be denied that my siblings and I—all of us abandoned by our birth mothers and fathers—later felt abandoned by our adopted mother, Pearl. It also cannot be denied that Carol played an unwitting role in our abandonment—if only because she was one of the primary impetuses that spurred my mother to write. My siblings and I are not close, nor did they know Carol, or anything about her life or the bond between Carol and myself. They always remained separate. Not because they did not care; only because my mother did not involve them in Carol's life. My younger siblings were almost seventeen years Carol's junior, and so had contact with her only during her brief summer visits to Pennsylvania. This was a world that they were not a part of, and were not ever expected to participate in, unless, of course, I preceded my sister in death.

I therefore write this Afterword not only to update the story of Carol's life, but also to explain the way my mother lived her life. In so doing, I hope that I might help my siblings and others familiar with my mother's life to understand what happened in the past. My brothers and sisters were often hurt by my mother's apparent aloofness, and did not understand how they fit into her life. The truth is, she did not intend to hurt them, but she needed to give meaning to her own life. And one of her primary methods of giving meaning to her life was to support those who were unable to speak for themselves—whether it be the minorities or oppressed peoples of the world, or those who were slow to learn, like my sister. As a public figure, she was able to reach out to all peoples of the world, and show her compassion and concern. She was able to leave a legacy of simple caring for all mankind who would listen and accept her challenge. Would this legacy have been different if she had not given birth to Carol? It is impossible to say for sure, of course, but I think that the answer is "yes."